The Imagery *of* Scripture

The Imagery *of* Scripture

Seeing the Word through New and Ancient Eyes

DAVID STELLWAGEN

RESOURCE *Publications* • Eugene, Oregon

THE IMAGERY OF SCRIPTURE
Seeing the Word through New and Ancient Eyes

Copyright © 2022 David Stellwagen. All rights reserved. Except for brief quotations in critical publications or reviews, no part of this book may be reproduced in any manner without prior written permission from the publisher. Write: Permissions, Wipf and Stock Publishers, 199 W. 8th Ave., Suite 3, Eugene, OR 97401.

Resource Publications
An Imprint of Wipf and Stock Publishers
199 W. 8th Ave., Suite 3
Eugene, OR 97401

www.wipfandstock.com

PAPERBACK ISBN: 978-1-6667-3640-3
HARDCOVER ISBN: 978-1-6667-9463-2
EBOOK ISBN: 978-1-6667-9464-9

MARCH 14, 2022 8:59 AM

Copyright Notices: NKJV

Scripture taken from the New King James Version®. Copyright © 1982 by Thomas Nelson. Used by permission. All rights reserved.

Scripture quotations taken from the 21st Century King James Version®, copyright © 1994. Used by permission of Deuel Enterprises, Inc., Gary, SD 57237. All rights reserved.

Any reference to a translation of Greek or Hebrew is taken from Young's Analytical Concordance to the Bible, by Robert Young, Eerdman's, 1979.

Images used are either considered public domain, were granted permission by owner, or were purchased for full use from Dreamstime.com & Alamy.com. All photos of the Klosterneuburg ambo are courtesy of Peter Böttcher, IMAREAL Krems, Austria.

*To the four ladies I love
And to a father who awaits our next meeting.*

The real voyage of discovery consists not in seeking new landscapes, but in having new eyes.

—MARCEL PROUST

Contents

Prologue | ix

1 Seeing is Everything | 1

2 Core Truth | 5

3 Lessons Learned | 8

4 The Death of Samson | 10

5 Two Sides | 14

6 The Sacrifice of Isaac | 24

7 The Burning Bush | 37

8 Grapes on a Pole | 43

9 Firsts | 48

10 Serpent | 55

11	Supreme Food	61
12	A Fish & A Coin	66
13	Unicorn	73
14	A Wee Little Man	76
15	Perfect Soul Vision	80
16	Water & Wine	86
17	The Twenty-third Psalm	89
18	The Ox & The Donkey	98

Epilogue | 105

Bibliography | 107

Prologue

EPIC JOURNEYS SOMETIMES BEGIN in the most unexpected places.

This Bible study started with a strange tree. In a chance encounter with an art book by Thomas Hoving, I became intrigued by an ivory cross carved almost a thousand years ago in England. Hoving believed this was one of the greatest works of art in the history of the world. I thought it was downright ugly.

The Cloisters Cross, 1150–60 AD,
courtesy of the Metropolitan Museum of Art, New York City.

PROLOGUE

But my curiosity was piqued. What was it about this work that made the former director of the Metropolitan Museum in New York City, one of the supreme art museums on the planet, think such a thing? I learned soon thereafter that Hoving had authored an entire book on the cross. Something prodded me to find out what he had to say. Maybe the book would change my mind.

Little did I know.

The name of the book is *King of the Confessors*, and its opening sentence reads, "In the spring of 1955, after eight centuries of silence, a mysterious work of art, one of the most beautiful and enigmatic ever created in world history, suddenly turned up in the hands of a strange and secretive collector."[1]

There it was again. A claim of grandeur that I simply did not see. I set out to read the book in its entirety. Within a few pages, Hoving had me hooked. I devoured it. But this was not your average read. Though it is a book focused on a work of art, its biblical implications are profound. Hoving writes, "There was so much to learn about the cross. A world. Virtually the significance of the Old and New Testaments."[2]

This book on the Cloisters Cross stated some church leaders of the Middle Ages believed that a relatively unknown verse from the Old Testament was a direct reference to Jesus and his crucifixion. The passage is from the Song of Songs (or the Song of Solomon), and it reads as follows (unless otherwise noted, every biblical quote will be taken from the New King James Version):

> Song of Songs 7:8 "I will go up to the palm tree, I will take hold of its branches."

I thought the interpretation that those words pointed to the crucifixion was a little extreme, but at the same time I was intrigued. What was it about this obscure verse that made some ancient church fathers believe those fifteen words pointed to how Jesus willingly went to the cross to suffer and die so that all who believe in him might be saved?

1. Hoving, *King of the Confessors*, 19.
2. Hoving, *King of the Confessors*, 81.

Prologue

My curiosity got the better of me, so I did two things:

1. I decided to give those church leaders of old the benefit of the doubt and consider the possibility that they were right that this passage was/is a direct reference to the Messiah and his cross;
2. I set out to do a little investigating to see what other biblical passages I could find in connection with a palm tree.

I found examples connected with Palm Sunday (in John 12:12–13), with Solomon's temple (in I Kings 6:29), and even in this unique verse:

> Psalm 92:12 "The righteous shall flourish like a palm tree."

After finding verses with palm trees potentially connected with the Messiah, I still wasn't convinced that those ancient church fathers were right; but I thought they might be on to something with their idea that an image from the Old Testament pointed to the Savior and the plan of salvation. I decided to research a few other images that I knew from past knowledge pointed to Jesus (i.e., lamb, rock, etc.) and turn it into a short family Bible study.

I can now easily picture God smiling at such an idea; for what I thought would turn out to be only a brief Bible study led me down a path I could not have imagined.

I ended up with over three hundred images, some of them basic, some of them grand; but the unexpected treasure of that search was that those images allowed me to see the stories of Scripture in an entirely different light. What I never imagined was that it would take thousands of hours of constant study and writing to work my way through the entire Bible.

The next step in my journey led to the classroom. As an eighth-grade teacher at a Christian school, I have had the great fortune to teach a variety of subjects. Through that experience I came to believe that educational subjects should blend and blur into each other as much as possible. Teaching U. S. History, literature, English, art, and religion offered a plethora of opportunities to achieve that ideal. When I eventually decided to share some of the stories with my students, I struggled with a relevant question: how do I best introduce the topic? Two decades of teaching experience revealed the need for something visual. Since my fledgling fascination with the art world was inseparably linked to the early stages of this study, I sensed it might be the perfect combination to meld and overlap. I took the leap.

The positive reaction, year after year, finally convinced me I should try sharing it with even a larger audience. Hence, the birth of this book.

So, allow me the privilege of showing you the riches I found after more than ten years of feasting upon the wonder and awe of God's Word.

1

SEEING IS EVERYTHING

Sherlock Holmes~George~Silence

WHAT DO YOU SEE?

Those four words form the crux of my teaching philosophy. They lay the foundation I ask my students to build upon daily. As a Christian educator, I strive to help my students see new things—things that will impact how they view their education, the world around them, and even God's Word.

Once I decided to share parts of this study with my students (and settled on using the art world to introduce it), I then faced the dilemma of which story or work of art to begin with. It didn't take long to find something that has proven highly effective.

What I'd like to do here is share with you that approach, to show you how I emphasize with those students the need to see things through fresh eyes.

During the first week of school, I show my students the following piece of art.

The Imagery of Scripture

Bernat Martorell, *Saint George and the Dragon*, 1434,
The Art Instititue of Chicago.

The work is a painting by the Spaniard, Bernat Martorell, which is over five hundred years old. (That makes it a bit older than my laminated poster.) At the beginning of the twenty-first century, two researchers, Lisa and Jeffrey Smith, found that the average time spent in front of a work of art at a museum is roughly twenty-seven seconds.

I ask my students (and now you, as well) to study the work for double that length: one minute. I turn it into a mini-Sherlock Holmes game. What details matter? The clues are there. Can they find them—can you? In the end, it all comes down to one thing:

What do you see?

Seeing is Everything

The students do their best to see as much in the painting as they can. Then it is time to open their eyes.

I tell the students that the warrior's name is George. He was a pagan who converted to Christianity later in life. George felt he had a calling to spread the Good News of the Gospel. Legend has it that one day, as he wandered into a new kingdom, he encountered a young maiden about to be devoured by a hideous dragon. George, being the stud-muffin he was (and yes, I call him a stud-muffin), felt he had no choice but to slay the dragon and save the girl, which is exactly what he did.

Little did he know that the damsel was no ordinary young lady. She was the only daughter of the king and queen and had been chosen by lottery that year to die. This was the only way to appease the wrath of the dragon that had plagued the kingdom for decades. In gratitude for saving his daughter, the king offered George the chance to marry the princess. George accepted. He had slain a dragon and won a one-of-a-kind bride in the process. Life . . . was . . . *good*.

But there's more to the story. Though this legendary battle never actually happened, the story was sometimes used by artists and the church as a picture (or image) of something that did occur around two thousand years ago. And it is here where I ask the students the question that the painting and its story have been leading to:

> How does the depth of the story change
> if George is seen as an image of Jesus?

Once they are told that George is an image of Jesus, it doesn't take long for one of them to state that the dragon must be an image of the devil. As soon as that connection is made, I read a Bible verse.

> Revelation 20:2 "He laid hold of the dragon, that serpent of old, who is the Devil and Satan . . . "

Just like that, the kids know they are on the right track—at which point I ask them what George used to slay the dragon in the painting. Inevitably, someone in the room connects the spear in the painting with the spear used to pierce Jesus' side. Eventually, someone also makes the connection that that spear was being used to defeat and conquer the devil (a.k.a. the dragon).

I ask them to look closely at the poster once again and tell me what they see on George's armor, namely, the breastplate with a red cross on a white background. Numerous students see and understand that the red points to the blood Jesus shed to win that battle and the white points to his purity.

The imagery of the princess is typically a little more difficult for the class, but more often than not, at least one of them realizes that she is an image of the church. When Jesus defeated the devil on Good Friday, he won something—a bride—which just happens to be the church. I head right back to Scripture.

> Ephesians 5:25 "Husbands, love your wives, just as Christ also loved the church and gave Himself for her."

Finally, I leave them with one more thought:

> Where do they think the idea came from to create a legendary story that pointed to Jesus as the conquering Savior of the world?

Believe it or not, there was an actual George who did spread the Gospel, but he didn't slay any dragon to win a bride. So, where did that idea come from? Every year, the reply is the same: silence.

I let the students (and now you as well) know that the answer is, without a doubt, one of the greatest things I have encountered in my life. I learned that one idea behind the fictitious tale of St. George slaying the dragon is founded on other stories that are works of truth, works that contain zero embellishment or mythical detail, stories that are found in Scripture. That is what this Bible study is all about—seeing those biblical stories through fresh (and possibly new) eyes.

2

Core Truth

Truth~39~The Floor

A QUICK QUIZ. One question. Pass or fail.
   What is the core truth of the Bible?
   It should come as no surprise that the Word provides the answer.

> I Corinthians 2:2 "For I determined not to know anything among you except Jesus Christ and Him crucified."

The truth? Everything revolves around Jesus and the cross at Calvary. It sounds so basic, so simplistic, so easy, but what I want to show you, step by step, is how deep and intricate that truth really is.
   In my classroom, the day after I show the students George and the Dragon, I present them with another work of art.
   If we were to walk into the National Gallery of Art in Washington, D.C., and enter room thirty-nine, I would ask you to look closely at a vertically narrow painting by a man named Jan van Eyck (pronounced Yahn vahn-Ike). The work by van Eyck is a depiction of what Christians usually refer to as the Annunciation, the moment when Gabriel announced the impending birth of the Messiah to Mary.

The Imagery of Scripture

Jan van Eyck, *The Annunciation*, 1434-35,
courtesy National Gallery of Art, Washingon.

Other than noting the incredible detail in the painting, especially that of Gabriel's robe, we might not give the painting a second glance.

But we'd be missing something supreme.

If we paused just a few seconds longer to look closely at the floor in van Eyck's painting, we'd notice that he painted some intricate scenes on the tiles. If we bent over and peered even closer, besides making the museum guards a little nervous, we'd see that the two clearest scenes depict the death of Samson and David killing Goliath.

Core Truth

And at that point we would be wise to ask a quick question: how might those two stories be connected to the announcement of Jesus' birth?

3

LESSONS LEARNED

Mistake~Write~Time

BEFORE WE BEGIN WITH OUR FIRST STORY, I would like to share two potentially significant insights with you.

The first is that experience has taught me that in order to fully grasp and comprehend something of importance, it is essential to write down both what you learned and your reaction to it. I wish I had jotted down my thoughts in a composition notebook or on a computer from day one of this study. I would love to go back and read what I was thinking as I came across various insights and stories.

I missed out on that—but hope that you learn from my mistake.

Secondly, this might sound strange, but I highly recommend that you do something perhaps unexpected: write in your Bible. As I progressed through this study, I realized that to comprehend the full impact of God's imagery in his Word, I wanted to see the big picture. To do that, I concluded I needed to mark the various imagery in a given section. I decided to mark all the images (person, place, or thing) I found in direct connection with Jesus and his atoning sacrifice by circling them.

Lessons Learned

As I moved further and further into this study, I was amazed at how abundant imagery is throughout Scripture—and the markings were the proof.

It's time. The initial ideas have been written and read. It's time to open the Word and see its wonders.

It's time.

4

THE DEATH OF SAMSON

Italics~Victory~Door Frame

SOME OF THE ANCIENT CHRISTIAN CHURCH LEADERS were enthralled with the man known as Samson. In this chapter, we will focus on Samson's demise.

> Judges 16:23–30 "Now the lords of the Philistines gathered together to offer a great sacrifice to Dagon their god, and to rejoice. And they said: 'Our god has delivered into our hands Samson our enemy!' When the people saw him, they praised their god; for they said: 'Our god has delivered into our hands our enemy, the destroyer of our land, and the one who multiplied our dead.' So it happened, when their hearts were merry, that they said, 'Call for Samson, that he may perform for us.' So they called for Samson from the prison, and he performed for them. And they stationed him between the pillars. Then Samson said to the lad who held him by the hand, 'Let me feel the pillars which support the temple, so that I can lean on them.' Now the temple was full of men and women. All the lords of the Philistines were there—about three thousand men and women on the roof watching while Samson performed. Then Samson called to the Lord, saying, 'O Lord God, remember me, I pray! Strengthen me, I pray, just this once, O God, that I

The Death of Samson

may with one blow take vengeance on the Philistines for my two eyes!' And Samson took hold of the two middle pillars which supported the temple, and he braced himself against them, one on his right and the other on his left. Then Samson said, 'Let me die with the Philistines!' And he pushed with all his might, and the temple fell on the lords and all the people who were in it. So the dead that he killed at his death were more than he had killed in his life."

It should come as no surprise that in these verses, *Samson* will serve as an image of Jesus. (From this point on we will italicize anyone or anything directly connected with Jesus as the *Savior*).

Let's see how that is the case.

*The unbelievers taunted and mocked *Samson*.

The Gospels tell us that Jesus endured the same thing.

Luke 23:35-36 "And the people stood looking on. But even the rulers with them sneered, saying, 'He saved others; let Him save Himself if He is the Christ, the chosen of God.' The soldiers also mocked Him . . . "

*The unbelievers didn't know it, but *Samson* was about to turn this mocking into a major victory.

This is something grand. As Jesus hung upon the cross on Good Friday, hardly anyone understood that he was in the process of winning a major victory over sin and the devil.

**Samson* willingly sacrificed his own life to conquer the unbeliever and protect his own people.

This is precisely what Jesus accomplished at Calvary.

After reading the verses of this story, we know that *Samson* pushed on the pillars of the temple of Dagon and destroyed both the building and its inhabitants; but what I want us to try and do is to visualize the body position of *Samson* just before that monumental event.

The Imagery of Scripture

Samson stood between the two pillars and prepared to push with all his might.

Try to envision where *Samson* placed his arms and hands to accomplish that feat. Stand in a doorway that is a little wider than normal. Imagine that the sides of the door frame are the two pillars between which *Samson* stood. Place your hands out from your body in order to gain the greatest leverage.

Now look at your body position and note how it is almost identical to someone else's body position: Jesus upon the cross. (For the best effect, turn your palms so they face forward instead of toward the imaginary pillars.)

And that leads us to another thought:

> Has anyone ever pondered what the pillars of Dagon's temple were made of?

If we open our Bibles to two short passages . . .

> I Kings 6:18 "The inside of the temple was cedar, carved with ornamental buds and open flowers. All was cedar; there was no stone to be seen."

> I Kings 7:1–2 "But Solomon took thirteen years to build his own house; so he finished all his house. He also built the House of the Forest of Lebanon . . . with four rows of cedar pillars, and cedar beams on the pillars."

. . . we see that the pillars of Solomon's palace and the inside of God's temple were made of wood. And since the Philistines lived in the same area of the world as the Israelites, it seems a logical possibility that the pillars of Dagon's temple were made of wood as well. And that means just before he died, not only were *Samson's* hands raised up, they were also in contact with wood, just like Christ's hands at the cross.

Samson was a judge who also happened to be a big-time sinner (man, was he ever); but what happened to him pointed to that ultimate Judge (see James 5:9) who would be without sin and who would also willingly sacrifice himself to destroy the house of the wicked and protect the believers (that's us).

The Death of Samson

Now that we see a connection between the story of Samson's death and the birth announcement of the coming Judge and Savior, we need to look at the other scene depicted on that floor that van Eyck painted: David slaying Goliath.

A DISCREPANCY

An interesting thing to note is that in his painting of the Annunciation, van Eyck depicted the imagery surrounding the death of *Samson* using a different (and erroneous) perspective, for in his work of art, he showed *Samson* pushing down only one pillar instead of two (which Scripture clearly indicates with the plurality of the noun). Van Eyck almost certainly chose to do this because a few of the early church leaders believed that the details of *Samson's* death pointed to when Jesus was scourged and flogged by the Romans on his way to being crucified.

The Bible clearly supports our view of the story and its connection with the cross, but either way, the detail still leads to Calvary.

5

Two Sides

Staff~Five~Elah

Even though it's rather lengthy, please skim I Samuel 17:1–37 to get a grasp of the story.

Before we look at specific verses in this section, we need to first note the obvious: that *David* throughout this chapter will serve as an image of the future Messiah while Goliath will continually serve as an image of the largest of all unbelievers, the devil. That's the basic imagery, but how God builds around it is exquisite.

Goliath taunted and challenged the Israelites. He was looking for a one-on-one battle to the death. Read his words carefully. (Note: we will continue to italicize any image of the future Savior, even within quotes from Scripture.)

> I Samuel 17:8 "... choose a *man* for yourselves, let him come down to me."

I wonder if Goliath had a clue as to what he was saying and how clearly it pointed to the future Messiah, the *man*, Jesus, who would "come down" from heaven (see John 6:32–35) to fight one on one with the devil at Calvary and conquer him, exactly like *David* was about to do with Goliath.

Two Sides

While we're on the topic of this *man*, we need to note a couple of things about this guy named *David*:

- He was a *shepherd*, a *protector* of his father's flock.
- He was a *defender* of God and his people (see verse thirty-six).

Both sound like a *man* named Jesus.

No matter how we look at it, this was to be a one-on-one battle of epic proportions. Goliath versus *David* . . . the devil versus the Son . . .

Are there any questions about who would be victorious?

FIVE SMOOTH STONES

I Samuel 17:38–47 "So Saul clothed *David* with his armor, and he put a bronze helmet on his head; he also clothed him with a coat of mail. *David* fastened his sword to his armor and tried to walk, for he had not tested them. And *David* said to Saul, 'I cannot walk with these, for I have not tested them.' So *David* took them off. Then he took his staff in his hand; and he chose for himself five smooth stones from the brook, and put them in a shepherd's bag, in a pouch which he had, and his sling was in his hand. And he drew near to the Philistine. So the Philistine came, and began drawing near to *David*, and the man who bore the shield went before him. And when the Philistine looked about and saw *David*, he disdained him; for he was only a youth, ruddy and good-looking. So the Philistine said to *David*, 'Am I a dog, that you come to me with sticks?' And the Philistine cursed *David* by his gods. And the Philistine said to *David*, 'Come to me, and I will give your flesh to the birds of the air and the beasts of the field!' Then *David* said to the Philistine, 'You come to me with a sword, with a spear, and with a javelin. But I come to you in the name of the Lord of hosts, the God of the armies of Israel, whom you have defied. This day the Lord will deliver you into my hand, and I will strike you and take your head from you. And this day I will give the carcasses of the camp of the Philistines to the birds of the

The Imagery of Scripture

air and the wild beasts of the earth, that all the earth may know that there is a God in Israel. Then all this assembly shall know that the Lord does not save with sword and spear; for the battle is the Lord's, and He will give you into our hands.'"

David killing Goliath is one of the best-known stories in all of Scripture. Almost everyone knows it, from the Sunday School child to the nursing home resident.

But there is a surprise. Look what *David* decided to take into battle.

I Samuel 17:40 "Then he took his *staff* in his hand . . . "

Once a person knows that everything leads to the cross, imagery can't get much easier.

And just in case you are wondering, every indication is that David kept this staff in his hand as he did battle with Goliath. How do we know? The giant tells us so himself.

I Samuel 17:43 "So the Philistine said to David, 'Am I a dog, that you come to me with *sticks*?'"

How many Christians know that *David* fought Goliath with a *staff* in his hand? But now that we are beginning to see and understand God's imagery, we understand it couldn't have been any other way, because it all points to Jesus' victory over the devil—a victory that was accomplished by another hand and another piece of wood.

But as awesome as that insight is, the other thing that *David* took into battle may be even more incredible.

I Samuel 17:40 "Then he took his *staff* in his hand; and he chose for himself five smooth *stones*."

Scripture makes it clear that a *stone* is inseparably linked with the Messiah and his atoning sacrifice. I Peter 2:4 tells us that Jesus is a living *stone* who was rejected by the unbeliever but chosen by God. Peter then quotes Isaiah 8:13-14, which points out that the Messiah and his sacrifice would be a *stone* of stumbling to the

Two Sides

unbeliever, for they would not be able to accept and believe its importance. Isaiah 28:6, on the other hand, points out how the Messiah and his atoning sacrifice would be both the foundation and corner*stone* of the church as well.

But it is the next detail that truly blew me away. In order to fully understand the imagery of what we are about to look at, let's follow a path we have traveled before and ask ourselves a question.

Why did *David* choose five smooth *stones*?

If everything in Scripture is there for a reason, what is the big deal about *David* choosing five *stones*? Why didn't he choose only one—showing total trust in God? Or a whole handful—making a "machine gun" sling shot? Why did he have to pick exactly five *stones*?

While we are currently focusing on the imagery of Scripture, we haven't even begun to touch on a whole separate area within this study; namely, the imagery of specific numbers within God's Word. Numbers are an absolute gold mine of imagery within Scripture, and beginning with the next book, we will begin an in-depth look at them.

But for now, let's focus on what we read here. The bottom line is that *David* chose *five stones* . . . because it leads us to the cross at Calvary.

Some of the earliest church leaders understood that the number *five* was directly connected with the Messiah's atoning sacrifice. "How so?" you may wonder. Well, answer this basic question:

> How many wounds did Jesus sustain upon the cross at Calvary?

Let's allow God's Word to provide us with the answer.

> Luke 24:39 [And Jesus said to the disciples] "Behold, My hands and My feet." (That Psalm 22:16 tells us were all pierced.)
>
> John 19:34 "But one of the soldiers pierced His side . . ."

Do the math.

The Imagery of Scripture

Two hands plus two feet and one side equal *five* wounds! Remember, everything about I Samuel seventeen points to the Messiah's victory over the devil at Calvary. But who would have ever guessed that choosing *five smooth stones* would have led there as well?

Five smooth stones . . .

    chosen by a *shepherd* . . .

        whose hand was in direct contact with a piece of *wood*.

You know what? Goliath didn't stand a chance against *David* any more than the devil did against Jesus.

THE CLASH

> I Samuel 17:48–51 "So it was, when the Philistine arose and came and drew near to meet *David*, that *David* hurried and ran toward the army to meet the Philistine. Then *David* put his hand in his bag and took out a *stone*; and he slung it and struck the Philistine in his forehead, so that the *stone* sank into his forehead, and he fell on his face to the earth. So *David* prevailed over the Philistine with a sling and a *stone*, and struck the Philistine and killed him. But there was no sword in the hand of *David*. Therefore *David* ran and stood over the Philistine, took his sword and drew it out of its sheath and killed him, and cut off his head with it. And when the Philistines saw that their champion was dead, they fled."

If we could insert a drum roll, this would be the perfect place to do so. Actually, a trumpet blast would probably be more appropriate. We are finally at the climax of this incredible chapter from God's Word.

In modern lingo—it was time to rumble . . . it was time to "bring it" . . . it was time for a one-on-one grudge match that would only end when one of the participants was dead. It was *David* versus Goliath. It was a mismatch of epic proportions, but not in the way everyone thought.

Two Sides

So let's see how God decided to wrap up what has amounted to some mind-boggling imagery.

> I Samuel 17:48 "So it was, when the Philistine arose and came and drew near to meet *David*, that *David* hurried and ran toward the army to meet the Philistine."

David faced overwhelming odds, and yet he ran to meet Goliath with complete confidence. *David* did not run from this battle; he willingly entered it alone; and that is classic Messiah imagery.

But to where did *David* run? Where exactly would he fight Goliath? Though these verses do not specifically say, God told us the name of the place earlier in the story, and you will never guess where it leads (okay, you probably know exactly where).

> I Samuel 17:19 "Now Saul and they and all the men of Israel were in the Valley of Elah, fighting with the Philistines."

When I began to work on the details of these verses, I was surprised that the impending battle didn't take place on a mountain (or even a hill). Instead, Goliath and *David* met in a valley called Elah. Since this battle would be to the death, this valley could be an image of the valley of death referred to in Psalm 23:4. But if everything in Scripture is there for a reason, why did *David* and Goliath fight at a place named Elah instead of a mountain?

Well, in English, Elah means... are you ready for this?... Elah means...

The oak *tree*.

Let's allow the apostle Peter to explain that imagery to us.

> Acts 5:30 [And Peter said] "The God of our fathers raised Jesus, whom you murdered by hanging Him on a *tree*."

Pause here a moment and envision a man sitting in a kitchen. Various books and a legal pad are on the table. The man reads, lost in his work—when suddenly, he stops. Time appears to stand still. His mouth opens slightly. There is only silence.

When I saw *Elah* for the first time, there were no words—there *are* no words—to describe the thoughts that swirled in my head as I tried to grasp what I had just learned. More than two decades later the memory is still vivid, and I am convinced it will continue to bring a smile to my face until the day I die.

Goliath and *David* were about to battle in a valley named after a *tree*? Remember what I said about "Goliath" not standing a chance?

> I Samuel 17:49 reveals that the *stone* that *David* slung hit Goliath in the forehead.

Why did that *stone* (of sacrifice) have to hit Goliath in the forehead? The ultimate unbeliever had to be struck in the head because God had stated in the Garden of Eden that it would be so.

> Genesis 3:15 [And God said to the serpent] " . . . [The Messiah] shall bruise your head."

Any questions?

Before we wrap up this story, there is one more thing we need to note about this victor who carried *five smooth stones* and a wooden *staff* into battle:

> Do you remember where this *shepherd* came from?

I Samuel 17:12, 58 remind us that *David* came from . . . Bethlehem.

    Exactly like a guy—
        named Jesus!

Preface: The Greek

His name was Domenikos Theotokopoulos.

You probably just said something along the lines of, "Say what?" So, try this and repeat after me: Doe-men-nuh-kos Thay-oh-toe-kawp-oh-lus. Yes, that is a mouthful, which is precisely why he had a nickname. Domenikos was a painter from the island of Crete who had a Greek name. When he traveled to Spain in 1577 to further his art career, the Spanish found his name as difficult to pronounce as you and I do—so they called him "El Greco," which means "the Greek." El Greco had a unique style of painting that contained elongated bodies and vibrant, metallic colors. Modern art students often feel comfortable with him because his style is so easy to recognize.

Our goal here is to use one of his works as an opening for this story. Study it closely.

El Greco, *The Cleansing of the Temple*, 1600,
courtesy of the Frick Musueum, New York City.

The scene El Greco depicted is when Jesus drove out the money changers from the temple.

> John 2:13–17 "Now the Passover of the Jews was at hand, and Jesus went up to Jerusalem. And He found in the temple those who sold oxen and sheep and doves, and the money changers doing business. When He had made a whip of cords, He drove them all out of the temple, with the sheep and the oxen, and poured out the changers' money and overturned the tables. And He said to those who sold doves, 'Take these things away! Do not make My Father's house a house of merchandise!' Then His disciples remembered that it was written, 'Zeal for Your house has eaten Me up.'"

It is highly symbolic that on the left side of the work we find the unbelievers, while the believers are located on the right. The reason behind that placement comes from Matthew 25:33, where on Judgment Day, we learn that Christ will place the sheep (a.k.a. believers) on his right hand of blessing, while the goats (a.k.a. unbelievers) will be on his left (the hand of cursing).

But we want to look even deeper into the painting. Sometimes little things lead to great discoveries.

Look closely at the walls in the background. El Greco painted two scenes, both of which have a direct connection with the overall theme of the story. Do you recognize either of the Bible stories depicted in smoke-like paint? On the left side, the side of the unbelievers, we find Adam and Eve being driven out of the Garden of Eden in the exact same way that Jesus expelled the unbelievers from the temple. On the right side, El Greco painted something that is more difficult to distinguish. If you look closely, you hopefully should be able to make out that the scene is that of Abraham about to sacrifice Isaac.

> And at this point we would be wise to do something that we have already done in connection with this Bible study: we need to ask ourselves a question.
>
>> What does the sacrifice of Isaac have to do with the believers in the painting?
>
> I hope you will find the answer enlightening.

6

THE SACRIFICE OF ISAAC

Chartres~Ets~Angel

To begin, read Genesis 22:1–14.

"Now it came to pass after these things that God tested Abraham, and said to him, 'Abraham!' And he said, 'Here I am.' Then He said, 'Take now your son, your only son Isaac, whom you love, and go to the land of Moriah, and offer him there as a burnt offering on one of the mountains of which I shall tell you.' So Abraham rose early in the morning and saddled his donkey, and took two of his young men with him, and Isaac his son; and he split the wood for the burnt offering, and arose and went to the place of which God had told him . . . So Abraham took the wood of the burnt offering and laid it on Isaac his son; and he took the fire in his hand, and a knife, and the two of them went together. But Isaac spoke to Abraham his father and said, 'My father!' And he said, 'Here I am, my son.' Then he said, 'Look, the fire and the wood, but where is the lamb for a burnt offering?' And Abraham said, 'My son, God will provide for Himself the lamb for a burnt offering.' So the two of them went together. Then they came to the place of which God had told him. And Abraham built an altar there and placed the wood in order; and he bound Isaac his son and laid him on the

The Sacrifice of Isaac

altar, upon the wood. And Abraham stretched out his hand and took the knife to slay his son. But the Angel of the Lord called to him from heaven and said, 'Abraham, Abraham!' So he said, 'Here I am.' And He said, 'Do not lay your hand on the lad, or do anything to him; for now I know that you fear God, since you have not withheld your son, your only son, from Me.' Then Abraham lifted his eyes and looked, and there behind him was a ram caught in a thicket by its horns. So Abraham went and took the ram, and offered it up for a burnt offering instead of his son. And Abraham called the name of the place, The-Lord-Will-Provide; as it is said to this day, 'In the Mount of the Lord it shall be provided.'"

We will take different approaches as we look at the different sections of Scripture within this study, but in this glimpse at God's Word, let's attempt to see the imagery by asking a series of questions.

*Who was Isaac?

In this story God makes it clear in verse two that Isaac was an only son, and as soon as we realize that an *only son* was to be sacrificed, even though he didn't deserve it, then it is obvious that *Isaac* serves as a crystal-clear image of the Messiah.

*Where was Abraham ordered to sacrifice *Isaac*?

Whenever possible, it's best to let God provide us with the answer. This is what he tells us:

> Genesis 22:2 [And God said to Abraham] "Take now your *son*, your *only son Isaac*, whom you love, and go to the land of Moriah, and offer him there as a burnt offering on one of the mountains . . . "

A sacrifice of an *only son* upon a mountain? That sure sounds like Calvary.

*What did *Isaac* carry in verse six?

The Imagery of Scripture

Once we understand that *Isaac* is a clear-cut image of the Messiah, then what we read in verse six becomes so simple to see, for *Isaac* carried the *wood* used in the upcoming sacrifice in the exact same way that Jesus carried the *wood* of his cross.

In the city of Chartres, France, resides a grand Gothic cathedral that is basically an entire building dedicated to the imagery of Scripture (some of it correct, some of it not).

Look at the following quote from a book about a window in that cathedral: "Abraham is a figure for God the Father, and Isaac prefigures God the Son. In other windows at Bourges [in France] and Canterbury [in England], in fact, Isaac is even depicted carrying a cross, whilst here [at Chartres] he carries the sticks for his sacrifice tied in two bundles, crossed so that the symbolism is implied."[1]

Since all three of those cathedrals were built hundreds of years ago, it is clear some of the church leaders of the Middle Ages saw and understood Genesis 22:6 perfectly.

Before we leave this imagery, we need to note one more thing; and it is something that reveals how incredibly important it is to see and ponder the Word of God in its original language.

The Hebrew word used in Genesis 22 for *wood* is "*ets*," and that is the exact same Hebrew word often translated in the Old Testament as *tree*. (See Deuteronomy 21:22 for a prime example.)

That translation (and connection) should sound familiar.

> Acts 5:30 [And Peter said] "The God of our fathers raised Jesus, whom you murdered by hanging on a *tree*."

> Galatians 3:13 "Christ has redeemed us from the curse of the law, having become a curse for us (for it is written, 'Cursed is everyone who hangs on a *tree*.')"

*What did Abraham say would be provided as the true sacrifice?

> Genesis 22:8 "And Abraham said, 'My son, God will provide for Himself the *lamb* for a burnt offering.'"

---

1. Miller, *Chartres Cathedral*, 51.

Abraham's word choice was/is nothing short of amazing once we realize that he used an image that is inseparably linked with the Savior: a *lamb*.

Let's pause for a moment and see where else we find this basic, straightforward image connected with the Messiah.

LAMB

> John 1:29 [And John the Baptist said when he saw Jesus] "**Behold!** The *Lamb* of God who takes away the sin of the world."

> John 1:35-36 "Again the next day, John stood with two of his disciples. And looking at Jesus . . . said, '**Behold** the *Lamb* of God.'"

Is there a Christian on earth who does not know this image of Jesus as the *lamb*?

Before we leave these words from John the Baptist, I'd like to point out something I learned long ago—how often words like **behold, indeed, look, see, assuredly, surely, truly**, etc., are directly connected with imagery of the Messiah. We will see it repeatedly as we work our way through this study. (And they will be bolded from now on for emphasis.)

Let's look where we find the image of a *lamb* in the Old Testament and how it pointed to the coming Savior.

In preparation for their exodus out of Egypt, look what was sacrificed at the first Passover:

> Exodus 12:3-5, 21 "On the tenth of this month every man shall take for himself a *lamb* . . . Your *lamb* shall be without blemish . . . Then Moses said, 'Pick out and take the *lambs* for yourselves according to your families and kill the Passover *Lamb*.'"

Then there's this example, one of the greater images of the Messiah as the "suffering servant:"

Isaiah 53:7 "He was oppressed and afflicted, yet He opened up not His mouth. He was led as a *lamb* to the slaughter."

Now look at this selection from the New Testament:

I Peter 1:18-19 "Knowing that you were not redeemed with corruptible things . . . but with the precious blood of Christ, as of a *lamb* without blemish and without spot."

Now do you see and understand why Abraham's word choice in Genesis 22:8 was so important? God would provide a *lamb* as the ultimate sacrifice; a *lamb* that would also be an *only son*—and his name would be Jesus.

Let's return to the scene recorded in Genesis twenty-two.

*Where did Abraham place *Isaac* in order to sacrifice him?

Look at what God tells us:

Genesis 22:9 " . . . And Abraham built an altar there and placed the *wood* in order; and he bound *Isaac* his *son* and laid him on the altar upon the *wood*."

Can imagery get any more similar to the cross at Calvary than that? And yes, the Hebrew word used for *wood* in verse nine is also "*ets*," which means that Genesis 22:9 could also correctly read:

"And Abraham laid him . . . upon the *tree*."

And that imagery is as easy as any we will encounter in this entire study.

*I think it is a logical question to ask what *Isaac* was doing during all this impending sacrifice preparation by Abraham.

If we look closely, we see that the Bible does not mention *Isaac* at all. Abraham bound *Isaac* and laid him on the altar, and yet Scripture doesn't record a single word uttered by *Isaac*. But why? The answer lies in the imagery, for Isaiah prophesied what the Messiah would be like during his sacrifice, and it is identical to *Isaac's* situation and behavior here in Genesis twenty-two.

Isaiah 53:7 "He was oppressed and He was afflicted, yet He opened not His mouth. He was led as a *lamb* to the slaughter, and as a *sheep* before its shearers is silent, so He opened not His mouth."

How are we doing so far? I'm guessing your "vision" is improving by the minute. But believe it or not, we're just getting warmed up, for this is where things get even more interesting.

Look who showed up as this mind-boggling imagery was unfolding.

Genesis 22:11 "But the Angel of the Lord called to [Abraham] . . . "

Before we can go any further in this chapter, we need to peek at who this Angel of the Lord is.

THE ANGEL OF THE LORD

One of the more interesting observations about the Old Testament is that the Second Person of the Trinity (a.k.a. the Son) appeared frequently in the form referred to as *the Angel of the Lord*. While this is not exactly an image like some of the others we will study, it is priceless in showing his presence in the Old Testament.

Let's see where he appears and put the pieces together to prove his identity.

Once Moses had led the children of Israel out of Egypt, when they reached Mount Sinai, God said to them:

Exodus 23:20, 23 "**Behold**, I send an *Angel* before you to keep you in the way and to bring you into the place which I have prepared . . . for My *Angel* will go before you . . . "

Doesn't that make perfect sense? Who but the future Messiah, the Second Person of the Trinity, the Son of God, would lead the believers into the Promised Land?

But probably the story that gives us the greatest insight into the identity of this *Angel of the Lord* is found in the book of Judges.

The Imagery of Scripture

The parents of the hero named *Samson* (remember him?) received a visitor who was something special.

Look at what God tells us:

> Judges 13:3, 6, 17–18 "*The Angel of the Lord* appeared to the woman and said to her, '**Indeed** now, you are barren . . . but you shall conceive and bear a son.' . . . [And she said to her husband named Manoah] 'A *Man of God* came to me and His countenance was like the countenance of *the Angel of God*, very awesome . . . ' Then Manoah said to *the Angel of the Lord*, 'What is Your name, that when Your words come to pass, we may honor You?' And *the Angel of the Lord* said to him, 'Why do you ask My name, seeing it is wonderful?'"

And to prove to us once and for all that this *Angel of the Lord* was no ordinary angel, look at what Manoah said later:

> Judges 13:22 "And Manoah said to his wife, 'We shall surely die, because we have seen **God**!'" (Emphasis mine)

The "*man*" connection mentioned by Manoah's wife strongly suggests that this is the Son of God, who will be true man and true God; but is there any solid proof? Look at a few other instances where *the Angel* is mentioned:

> Psalm 34:7 "*The Angel of the Lord* encamps all around those who fear Him. And delivers them."

Who delivers the believer? None other than the Son.

> Psalm 35:5–6 "Let [the unbeliever] be like chaff before the wind, and let *the Angel of the Lord* chase them. Let their way be dark and slippery, and let *the Angel of the Lord* pursue them."

Who judges and condemns the unbeliever? Once again, the Son.

But it is the prophet Isaiah who leaves no doubt as to the identity of this *Angel*.

> Isaiah 63:8-9 "So He became their Savior. In all their affliction He was afflicted. And *the Angel of His Presence* saved them."

Who is the Savior? Who was afflicted by our affliction (see Isaiah fifty-three)? The Son. And his name is Jesus.

So, think about what we have in Genesis twenty-two up to this point:

> In verses 1-10 we have one of the grandest stories of imagery in the entire Bible, imagery that clearly leads us nowhere else but to the cross at Calvary, and look who showed up—the Second Person of the Trinity, the (only) Son of God, the *Lamb* of God, *the Angel of the Lord*.

And the best thing I can say to that is:

> Could it be any other way?

Let's head back to the twenty-second chapter of Genesis and see how the story and its imagery progresses.

> In Genesis 22:13 we read, "And there behind him was a *ram* caught in a thicket by its horns. So Abraham went and took the *ram* and offered it up for a *burnt offering* instead of his son."

The shift here in imagery is swift. Isaac now becomes an image of every believer while the *ram* now serves an image of Jesus, who was sacrificed in our place. He suffered the Father's wrath so that we wouldn't have to.

*Genesis 22:13 tells us that the *ram* was caught in a thicket by its horns.

Let me ask a quick question about those details.

What is a thicket?

A thicket is a group of bushes or trees that often have some sort of sharp points connected with them. That idea of *wood* and sharp points (linked with the ram's head) leads us directly back to the atoning sacrifice of the Messiah.

The Imagery of Scripture

Matthew 27:29 "When they had twisted a *crown of thorns*, they put it on His head."

Abraham seemingly understood this imagery so well that we read in God's Word:

Genesis 22:14 "Abraham called the name of the place, The-Lord-Will-Provide, as it is said to this day, 'In the Mount of the Lord it shall be provided.'"

Abraham's word choice is also a perfect fit for Calvary. Think about the complete details of this chapter:

An innocent *only son* who was to be sacrificed on *wood* is inseparably linked with a *mount* named God-Will-Provide.

Imagery cannot get much richer than that.

There's one more thing I'd like to point out in connection with these grand verses, and I've saved it for last because it is inseparably connected with where this study began for me.

When God tells us that *Isaac* and the *ram* were to be "offered up" as a sacrifice, the Hebrew word used is "*alah*," and look where else we find the same Hebrew root word:

Song of Songs 7:8 [And the Messiah said] "I will **go up** ["*alah*"] into the *palm tree*. I will take hold of its *branches*." (Emphasis mine)

Picture, once again, a man, sitting at a kitchen table. He stops suddenly, frozen, stunned into silence. When I saw for the first time that *Isaac's* sacrifice was linked to the *palm tree* through an identical Hebrew verb, I didn't know what to do, or say, or think. It may seem like a minor detail, but it suddenly made for me the Song of Songs 7:8 a verse of force.

Little did I know this was only the tip of the iceberg.

THE SACRIFICE OF ISAAC
THROUGH ANCIENT EYES

What is equally stunning is that some of the ancient church fathers clearly understood much of this imagery. In the Middle Ages, something called the Biblia Pauperum (Bib-lee-ah Pow-per-room) was organized. This book was supposedly for the poor and consisted of woodblock prints put together with Bible passages containing imagery. This is what the Biblia Pauperum has to say about the sacrifice of *Isaac*: "We read in Genesis 22:6 that when Abraham and Isaac set out together, Abraham carried the sword and the fire, but Isaac the wood by which he was himself to be sacrificed; this Isaac who carried the wood is a type of Christ, who carried on His own body the wood of the cross on which He meant to be sacrificed for us."[2]

How's that for some major-league understanding that is hundreds of years old?

One of the many things I learned in this Bible study is how ignorant I was regarding the wisdom of various ancient church fathers. Read the words of Augustine, a man who lived around sixteen hundred years ago: "All things proclaim newness, and the new covenant is shadowed forth in the old. For what does the term old covenant imply but the concealing of the new? And what does the term new covenant imply but the revealing of the old?"[3]

In that wordy quote, Augustine tells us that the Old Testament concealed the New Testament and that the New Testament revealed the Old. Prior to this study, I would have assumed he was simply writing about prophecy; but now I understand that it includes imagery as well.

These men knew. They knew that the Old Testament was imagery of the New Testament, and the New Testament was a fulfillment of the Old Testament imagery. They would refer to this idea as typology (tie-pol-low-gee), instead of imagery, but other than that, they saw many of the things we will be studying, and we will reference them whenever possible.

2. Peterson, "What was the Biblia Pauperum" *d*.
3. Saint Augustine, *The City of God*, 549.

The Imagery of Scripture

But if that is the case, we need to ask ourselves a question: if this idea of imagery in Scripture has been known for centuries, why haven't we heard much about it, if we've heard anything at all?

The answer can be traced in part back to the Middle Ages and what had happened to people's vision regarding imagery:

> "In the Middle Ages many thought the Old Testament announced the coming of Christ in clear and prophetic words, but also that each event, each character, and each act in the New Testament had an allegorical [imagery] correspondence prefiguring it in the Old Testament. [But] in search for such correspondences between the Old Testament and New Testament, **medieval scholars clearly became a bit carried away in their bent for symbols and allegories.**"[4](Emphasis mine)

Some of the ancient church fathers lost focus. They used imagery to go on tangents that were never intended for it. In simple terms, the imagery of Scripture must point to what Scripture itself points to: namely, the fact that salvation comes through Jesus alone, not through any other means. Any imagery that contradicts that foundation of God's holy Word is false. We will elaborate on this idea later, but for now, let's simply marvel at the fact that the imagery of Scripture has been a known entity for almost two thousand years.

And that means it is time to move on to our next story.

---

4. Minne-Serve and Kergall, *Romanesque & Gothic France: Art & Architecture*, 278.

THE SACRIFICE OF ISAAC

NICHOLAS OF VERDUN

In Europe there is a religious work of art that is equally stunning. In the twelfth century AD, an artist by the name of Nicholas of Verdun (a city in France) constructed an ambo for the Klosterneuburg (Close-ter-noy-burk) monastery located just outside of Vienna, Austria. This ambo was like a pulpit from which a minister would preach. It had three sides, with the backside left open to allow entrance by the preacher. The entire ambo contains seventeen columns of plaques with three rows in each column (yielding fifty-one plaques in all). The top and bottom of each column depict Old Testament events, while the middle plaque depicts the New Testament event they pointed to.

Here is what it looks like.

Nicholas of Verdun, *The Klosterneuburg ambo*, 1171–81, courtesy of Dreamstime.com.

If we look closer at the main section, we see that at the top of the central column is a depiction of Isaac's sacrifice. Directly below it we find none other than the crucifixion of Jesus (which also happens to be the very center of the entire work of art;

35

an insight that should not be missed because it emphasizes that the entire focus of Scripture is Jesus on the cross).

Nicholas of Verdun, *The Klosterneuburg ambo*, 1171–81, courtesy of Klosterneuburg abbey.

It is remarkable to ponder that this artwork is over eight hundred years old, revealing how much some of the old church leaders (and the artists they hired) understood regarding the imagery of Scripture.

7

THE BURNING BUSH

Peter & Paul~Count~Tears

IN OUR PREVIOUS STORY we saw that it was the Son of God (as *the Angel of the Lord*) who spoke to Abraham on the mountain as he was about to sacrifice Isaac. Armed with that knowledge, this next story becomes much clearer.

The story of the burning bush is easily one of the best known in God's holy Word, but there is more to it than initially meets the eye.

Let's look at the actual story from Scripture (with our imagery markings added in):

> Exodus 3:1–5 "Now Moses was tending the flock of Jethro his father-in-law, the priest of Midian. And he led the flock to the back of the desert, and came to Horeb, the mountain of God. And *the Angel of the Lord* appeared to him in a *flame* of *fire* from the midst of a *bush*. So he looked, and **behold**, the *bush* was burning with *fire*, but the *bush* was not consumed. Then Moses said, 'I will now turn aside and *see* this great sight, why the *bush* does not burn.' So when the Lord saw that he turned aside to look, God called to him from the midst of the *bush* and said, 'Moses, Moses!' And he said, 'Here I am.' Then He said,

'Do not draw near this place. Take your sandals off your feet, for the place where you stand is holy ground.'"

This surprised me when I first read it. I'm convinced that if we asked a hundred Christians which member of the Trinity spoke from the burning bush, at least ninety of them would say the Father or the Holy Spirit.

And they'd be wrong.

The Bible is clear: it was the future Messiah, the Son of God, *the Angel of the Lord*, who spoke to Moses from the *burning bush*. And that insight makes a world of difference when we look at the imagery contained within this story.

The entire foundation for the story rests on this point:

The *burning bush* serves as an image of the cross.

Let's look at all the intricacies of these five verses from the third chapter of Exodus that point to the *burning bush* as an image of the cross.

- The Hebrew word used in these verses for *bush* is "*seneh*." This Hebrew word is used to describe the thorny bush that grew in the barren areas of the Middle East. The plant was considered the lowliest of all plants in the area because it produced only thorns. This is a perfect fit for an image of the cross. The lowliness of the thorn *bush* is a complement to the humility that Christ displayed and endured while on the cross. (We also shouldn't miss the imagery connected with the *crown of thorns*.)

- Though we didn't go further in these verses from this story in Exodus, the Son told Moses from the *bush* that it was time for the children of Israel to be delivered from their slavery in Egypt. In contrast, Christ's message from the cross was that it was now time for his children (that's us) to be delivered from their slavery to sin.

But why did the *bush* burn with *fire* and what imagery does it contain? The answer comes in a variety of insights.

There are two main reasons that *fire* is connected with the *burning bush* and its imagery of the cross:

- *Fire* was an essential item in sacrificing *burnt offerings* to the Lord. A *sacrifice* was set on *fire* because then the smoke and aroma of the *burnt offering* ascended heavenward toward God. (This is exactly why God told Abraham to kill *Isaac* and offer him as a *burnt offering* in Genesis 22:2.)
- Throughout Scripture, *fire* is consistently connected with God's wrath (see Genesis 19:23–25 as one example), something the Savior would suffer upon the cross in order to atone for sin.

But there's more. Much more.

God tells us that the *fire* did not consume the *bush*. And that fact leads us to an important question:

Why not?

To answer that question, the first thing we need to note is two verses that we have already encountered.

> Acts 5:30 [And Peter said] "The God of our fathers raised Jesus, whom you murdered by hanging on a *tree*."

> Galatians 3:13 "Christ has redeemed us from the curse of the law, having become a curse for us (for it is written, 'Cursed is everyone who hangs on a *tree*.')"

Through divine inspiration, God made sure that the apostles Peter and Paul wrote that the cross was also a *tree*; and that insight has incredible meaning regarding the *burning bush*.

Scripture tells us that the *bush* was not consumed because God was giving Moses (and us) an image of what the cross at Calvary is all about.

In the Garden of Eden, Adam and Eve ate of the original Tree of Life, and it gave them life eternal; but when they sinned, they were driven from the Garden and prevented from eating of that very tree (see Genesis 3:22–24).

Jesus came to rectify that situation. When he climbed onto the *tree/bush* that is the cross, Jesus turned that piece of *wood* into the new *Tree of Life*. Jesus is the "fruit" of this new *Tree of Life* that we eat every time we partake of the Lord's Supper—and it brings eternal life in the same way that first tree in Eden did to Adam and Eve.

While the sacrifice of Jesus was accepted by the Father, the *Tree of Life* and its *fruit* endures forever. The *fire* of God's wrath would not totally devour the Son, for he would rise again on the third day and provide the world living proof that the *fruit* of his body (and the *Tree of Life*) would be available for eternity to all who truly believe. The *burning bush* that was not consumed is an incredible image of this very fact.

*All this is confirmed by the Lord himself in Exodus 3:5 when he said to Moses, "The place where you stand is holy ground."

The ground was holy because Moses was standing in front of an image of the cross, which also is exactly why this *burning bush* was found on a mount: because that is where the cross would be found as well.

*Exodus 3:7 ingeniously connects the Messiah with the *burning bush*/cross when God said about the believers, "For I know their sorrows."

The Hebrew word used here for sorrows ("*makhob*") leads us directly to a prophecy about Jesus' passion and suffering.

> Isaiah 53:3–4 "He is despised and rejected by men, a man of sorrows ["*makhob*"] and acquainted with grief. And we hid, as it were, our faces from Him. He was despised and we did not esteem Him. Surely He has borne our griefs and carried our sorrows ["*makhob*"]."

*Exodus 3:8 further connects the *burning bush*/cross with the Messiah when it says, "So I [the Son] have come down to deliver them."

The Burning Bush

Compare those words of the Son of God from the *burning bush* with the words of Jesus while he dwelt bodily on earth.

> John 3:13 [And Jesus said] "No one has ascended to heaven but He who came down from heaven, that is, the Son of Man who is in heaven."

And where would the children of Israel be delivered to? To the Promised Land of course, just like you and I will one day be delivered to the Promised Land of heaven.

There is an incredible lesson to be learned from this grand story of the *burning bush* and it is directly connected to our study on the imagery of Scripture. The lesson to be learned revolves around Moses' behavior:

> Exodus 3:3-4 "Then Moses said, 'I will turn aside and **see** this great sight.' So when the Lord saw that he turned aside to **look**, God called to him . . . " (Emphasis mine)

Moses willingly chose to stop what he was doing to see the wonder and awe of God. When he did this, God spoke directly to him.

That is exactly where we stand as well. We have willingly chosen to use this study on imagery as an opportunity to see the wonder and awe of God's Word. As we progress, God speaks to us through the majesty of his imagery.

This study is all about seeing and understanding. We want to learn to see things through the eyes of men like Moses and Abraham. The further we proceed in this study, the closer we move to obtaining true 20/20 vision.

May the Lord grant us his wisdom as we strive to see what wonders his Word contains.

Behold, the wonder and awe of God's Word.

But guess what?

There is one more thing we need to note regarding the imagery of this story, and it is something that will be difficult for me to forget. Ever.

The further I moved forward in this Bible study, the more I became convinced that it was vital to obtain as close a literal

The Imagery of Scripture

translation of the Old Testament Hebrew and the New Testament Greek as possible.

> Exodus 3:1–5 "Now Moses was tending the flock of Jethro his father-in-law, the priest of Midian. And he led the flock to the back of the desert, and came to Horeb, the *mountain* of God. And *the Angel of the Lord* appeared to him in a *flame* of *fire* from the midst of a *bush*. So he looked, and **behold**, the *bush* was burning with *fire*, but the *bush* was not consumed. Then Moses said, 'I will now turn aside and see this great sight, why the *bush* does not burn!' So when the Lord saw that he turned aside to look, God called to him from the midst of the *bush* and said, 'Moses, Moses!' And he said, 'Here I am.' Then He said, 'Do not draw near this place. Take your sandals off your feet, for the place where you stand is holy ground.'"

Here is what I'd like you to do: reread those verses and count the number of times that the word *bush* appears. (You should be made aware that after verse five, the word *bush* doesn't appear again in the entire story.)

How many?

Five.

And I have a funny feeling that you know what is coming next.

> Why did God have the Hebrew word for *bush*
> appear precisely *five* times in this story?

Hmmm . . . what does the number *five* have to do with the crucifixion?

Psssst—

Think . . .

Wounds.

I can only hope and pray that you are as stunned by that connection as much as I was the first time I encountered it.

Do you remember that man sitting at the kitchen table, working on this study? He was almost in tears (of joy) at this point.

8

GRAPES ON A POLE

Augustine~Cut Down~Robbers

BEFORE WE PROCEED IN THIS CHAPTER, we need to backtrack a little bit.

In our look at the imagery found in the sacrifice of *Isaac*, we mentioned that the art/religious object referred to as the Klosterneuburg (Close-ter-noy-burk) ambo in Austria depicted the sacrifice in direct connection with Jesus' crucifixion.

Well, there is a third plaque in that column of artwork that some of the ancient church fathers believed pointed to Good Friday as well, and it comes from a single verse in the Old Testament. Before we look at that verse however, it would be wise for us to understand the setting. After the children of Israel left their slavery in Egypt, twelve spies were sent into the Promised Land to scope it out and report what they found. While there, the following details were recorded:

> Numbers 13:23 "Then they came to the Valley of Eshcol, and there cut down a *branch* with one *cluster* of *grapes*; they carried it between two of them on a *pole* . . . "

You could probably tell where we are headed with this imagery as soon as you saw the italicized words, but let's dissect it anyway.

The Imagery of Scripture

A great place to start would be with a quote from an art book that states, "When Augustine [around 400 AD] declared that 'Jesus is the cluster of grapes of the Promised Land' . . . he was identifying Christ with the bunch of grapes brought back on a staff by the Hebrew spies who Moses had sent . . . The grapes on a staff recommended [pointed to] themselves as an image of the crucified Christ on the cross."[1]

The *cluster of grapes* recorded in Numbers 13:23 presents a treasure of imagery in connection with the future Savior.

Look at these two Old Testament passages that point to Jesus and his atoning sacrifice.

> Isaiah 65:8 "As the new *wine* is found in the *cluster*, and one says, 'Do not destroy it, for a blessing is in it . . .'"

> Song of Songs 7:7-8 [And the Messiah said to his bride] "This stature of yours is like a *palm tree*, and your breasts [which provide spiritual milk] like its *clusters*. I said, 'I will go up to the *palm tree*. I will take hold of its *branches*.'"

The *cluster of grapes* that came from the Promised Land foreshadowed the opportunity each and every believer would have to feast upon the Messiah both at the Lord's Table and in the Promised Land of paradise.

Numbers 13:23 tells us that the spies cut down a *branch* with one *cluster of grapes*.

Sometimes I simply marvel at how this study on imagery makes even the most basic of statements in Scripture marvelous. When we look at Numbers 13:23 through "old eyes," we see how basic the fact is that the spies cut down a branch of grapes because they wanted to take it back with them to show the people. But look at what we see when we look at this act through the eyes of imagery.

The Hebrew word used in verse twenty-three for to cut down is "*karath*," and that Hebrew word leads us to a clear image of the Messiah's passion and how he too would be "cut down."

---

1. Finaldi, *The Image of Christ*, 186.

Grapes on a Pole

> Jeremiah 11:19 "But I was like a docile *lamb* brought to the slaughter, and I did not know that they had devised schemes against Me, saying, 'Let us destroy the *Tree* [of *Life*] with its *fruit*, and let us **cut** Him **off** ["*karath*"] from the land of the living, that His name may be remembered no more.'"

Think about the magnitude of that single verse: the Messiah is directly connected with the *Tree of Life* that we mentioned previously, and he is also directly connected with the cut off *grapes* recorded in Numbers 13:23.

And what did the spies do with this *cluster of grapes*? They hung it on a *pole*. And what is a *pole* made of?

Why, wood of course . . .

Just like the beam of a cross.

But looking through the eyes of imagery allows us to see even more.

After the spies cut down the *branch*, they put it between two men, one on the right and one on the left. If that doesn't sound familiar, ponder the following verses carefully.

> Matthew 27:37–38 "And they put up over His head the accusation written against Him: This is Jesus the King of the Jews. Then two robbers were crucified with Him, one on the right and another on the left."

That connection leaves me with a question that I hope and pray I get the opportunity to ask once I sit at the feet of the Master Teacher: since Luke 23:39–43 reveals that one of the criminals cursed Jesus while the other one believed in him, does that tell us something about the two people who carried the *grapes* in Numbers thirteen? Could it be that one of the men was either Caleb or Joshua (the only two believers among the spies) and the other was one of the ten unfaithful, unbelieving spies? I can only wonder . . .

Behold, the wonder and awe of *grapes* on a *pole*, and how that *fruit* points in a myriad of ways to Jesus' atoning sacrifice for you and me.

All of it found in just a single verse of the Old Testament.

THE IMAGERY OF SCRIPTURE

GREEN

Here is the plaque of *grapes* on a *pole* as depicted by Nicholas of Verdun.

Nicholas of Verdun, *The Klosterneuburg ambo*, 1171–81, courtesy of Klosterneuburg abbey.

Don't forget, the scene above this is of the crucifixion. And above that? The sacrifice of Isaac.

But a different art example is equally grand. It comes from a stained-glass window in Chartres Cathedral (located in France).

Chartres Cathedral, courtesy of Dreamstime.com.

The scene at the top center is obviously the crucifixion. And directly below it? None other than a depiction of the two spies carrying the grapes.

But there's more.

Look closely at the cross that Jesus carries. What color is it? Wouldn't you expect it to be brown, the color of wood? So why is it green? The answer lies imbedded in the imagery we learned in connection with the *burning bush*, namely, that the cross became the new, green *Tree of Life*.

9

FIRSTS

Ground~Mark~Ghent

FIRSTS ARE MEMORABLE.

First day of school. First date. First kiss.

But what about the firsts that aren't so uplifting? Later in this study we will take time to see how important firsts can be in God's Word; but for now, let's focus on just two:

The first murder.

The first death.

Please read Genesis 4:1–15.

> "Now Adam knew Eve his wife, and she conceived and bore Cain . . . Then she bore again, this time his brother Abel. Now Abel was a keeper of sheep, but Cain was a tiller of the ground. And in the process of time it came to pass that Cain brought an offering of the fruit of the ground to the Lord. Abel also brought of the firstborn of his flock and of their fat. And the Lord respected Abel and his offering, but He did not respect Cain and his offering. And Cain was very angry, and his countenance fell. So the Lord said to Cain, 'Why are you angry? And why has your countenance fallen? If you do well, will you not be accepted? And if you do not do well, sin lies at the door. And its desire is for you, but you should rule over

it.' Now Cain talked with Abel his brother; and it came to pass, when they were in the field, that Cain rose up against Abel his brother and killed him. Then the Lord said to Cain, 'Where is Abel your brother?' He said, 'I do not know. Am I my brother's keeper?' And He said, 'What have you done? The voice of your brother's blood cries out to Me from the ground. So now you are cursed from the earth, which has opened its mouth to receive your brother's blood from your hand. When you till the ground, it shall no longer yield its strength to you. A fugitive and a vagabond you shall be on the earth.' And Cain said to the Lord, 'My punishment is greater than I can bear! Surely You have driven me out this day from the face of the ground; I shall be hidden from Your face; I shall be a fugitive and a vagabond on the earth, and it will happen that anyone who finds me will kill me.' And the Lord said to him, 'Therefore, whoever kills Cain, vengeance shall be taken on him sevenfold.' And the Lord set a mark on Cain, lest anyone finding him should kill him."

Cain murdering his brother Abel is another well-known Bible story. But what most people do not realize is that the story contains imagery of how the Pharisees would plot to kill Jesus.

Let's see how the details of the story point to that fact.

*The closer we look, the clearer it will become that Cain is clearly an image of the Pharisees.

Cain brought an offering that was unacceptable to the Lord. This is exactly like the Pharisees who thought they could earn their way to heaven. And just like Cain, they became irate when Jesus repeatedly informed them that they would never inherit the kingdom of God with such thinking.

Let's look at one such example from the Gospels. Watch closely for how similar it sounds to the circumstances surrounding Cain's offering in Genesis.

> Matthew 15:7-9, 12-13 [And Jesus said to the scribes and Pharisees] "Hypocrites! Well did Isaiah prophesy about you, saying, 'These people draw near to Me with

The Imagery of Scripture

their mouth, and honor Me with their lips, but their heart is far from Me. And in vain they worship Me'" . . .

[Then his disciples came and said to Jesus] "Do You know that the Pharisees were offended when they heard this saying?"

[But Jesus answered and said] "Every plant which My heavenly Father has not planted will be uprooted."

Clearly, Cain's offering was not acceptable to God because it did not come from a humble heart.

*Genesis 4:8 tells us that before Cain killed Abel, he talked with him.

We are not told what they spoke about, but the imagery points to the numerous conversations the Pharisees had with Jesus. And wherever we find those discussions in the Gospels, we see that the more they spoke with him, the angrier the Pharisees became. In fact, they became so angry that they resorted to plotting murder, just as Cain did regarding Abel.

*ced*Abel* is an image of Jesus.

The Bible describes *Abel* as a "keeper of the sheep." Not surprisingly, the Hebrew word used here is *"raah,"* the exact same word used for *shepherd*. This *keeper* of the sheep has an obvious connection with the Messiah:

> Psalm 23:1 "The Lord is my *shepherd* ["*raah*"]."

> Ezekiel 34:23 "I will establish one *shepherd* ["*raah*"] over them, and He shall feed them—My servant *David*. He shall feed them and be their *shepherd* ["*raah*"]."

Abel came before the Lord with a humble heart. This humble heart presented an acceptable sacrifice, just as Jesus' humble sacrifice would be acceptable to his Father to atone for all sin.

God was pleased with *Abel's* attitude, just as he was pleased with his Son's. And what was the result of God's approval? Cain hated *Abel* and eventually killed him, just as the Pharisees hated Jesus and killed him as well.

There are other details that connect Cain/*Abel* with the Pharisees/Jesus.

*How did Cain kill *Abel*?

If we read closely, we see that the actual act of murder isn't recorded in Scripture—but we can deduce some details: 1.) Genesis 4:8 tells us that Cain slew *Abel* "in the field" and 2.) God also tells us that the voice of *Abel's* blood cried out to him from the ground.

Abel's blood spilling upon the ground is incredibly meaningful.

First, it pointed to how Jesus' blood would also fall upon the ground as he hung upon the cross. Second, the blood falling upon the ground symbolically pointed to how Jesus' atoning blood would fall upon us, since we are made from the dust of the ground (see Genesis 2:7).

Those are details we should not miss.

*Genesis 4:15 tells us that after God announced his judgment on Cain, God placed a mark on him.

The Hebrew word used here for the mark is "*oth*," which also means "sign." Let's peek at some passages to see if we can determine what kind of sign God put on Cain.

> Exodus 12:13 [In connection with the Exodus out of Egypt, God says to the children of Israel] "Now the blood [of the *lamb*] shall be a *sign* ["*oth*"] for you on the houses where you are."

> Isaiah 7:14 "Therefore the Lord Himself will give you a *sign* ["*oth*"]: **Behold**, the virgin shall conceive and bear a Son, and shall call His name Immanuel."

God does not tell us exactly what mark he put on Cain, but it is clear from the Hebrew word that there is the distinct possibility that the *sign* was directly connected with the Savior.

I have read on a few occasions that some Bible scholars from the Middle Ages were convinced that the *mark* God put upon Cain was the *mark* of the cross. While there is no solid proof to confirm such a belief, everything else we've studied agrees with such a

The Imagery of Scripture

premise. It is also highly relevant because it confirms the teaching that Jesus died for everyone.

God placing this *sign/mark* upon Cain has great significance to every sinner. If God wanted even a murderer like Cain to see that the salvation of the cross was available to even him, surely that message applies to every other sinner as well. Even the Pharisees who condemned and murdered Jesus could have repented of their sin and received the mercy that is inseparably linked with the cross. And if God could forgive the men who killed his only begotten Son, surely he can forgive anyone who comes to him with a humble heart.

Behold, the wonder and awe of the first murder (and the first recorded death) and how it foreshadowed how the Pharisees would murder a *shepherd*, who turned out to be the Savior of the world.

GHENT

One of the greatest paintings in the history of Western art contains this imagery as well. In the city of Ghent, Belgium, is an altarpiece painted by the van Eyck brothers (yes, the same van Eyck we have already encountered). The realism and detail of the masterpiece are almost beyond human description; but just as we saw with the painting by El Greco, the easy-to-miss minor details often yield great treasure.

Hubert and Jan van Eyck, *The Ghent altarpiece*, , 1422–1432, courtesy of Alamy.com.

The altarpiece consists of twelve separate panels, each of which is a masterpiece in and of itself. The largest panel, found in the center of the bottom row is sometimes referred to as the Mystic Lamb. Jesus, as the Lamb of God, stands upon an altar as its blood flows into a chalice.

Sensory overload, though, might cause us to miss something essential to this study. If we slow down and look closely at the work, we might notice that in the upper corners of the

The Imagery of Scripture

altarpiece (above Adam on the left and Eve on the right) there are two separate quarter circles that depict parts of the same story: the offerings of Cain and Abel along with Cain murdering his brother, Abel.

10

SERPENT

Berea~John 3:16~Alan

WHEN YOU THINK OF the Bible and the image of a serpent (or snake), what pops into your head? Most people probably think of Satan in the Garden of Eden, when, as a serpent, he seduced Eve to eat the forbidden fruit.

But there is a different image connected with the serpent as well.

> Numbers 21:5-9 "And the people spoke against God and against Moses, 'Why have you brought us up out of Egypt to die in the wilderness? For there is no food and no water, and our soul loathes this worthless bread.' So the Lord sent fiery serpents among the people, and they bit the people, and many of the people of Israel died. Therefore the people came to Moses, and said, 'We have sinned for we have spoken against the Lord and against you; pray to the Lord that He take away the serpents from us.' So Moses prayed for the people. Then the Lord said to Moses, 'Make a *fiery serpent*, and set it on a *pole*; and it shall be that everyone who is bitten, when he looks at it, shall live.' So Moses made a *bronze serpent* and put it on a *pole*. And so it was, if a serpent had bitten anyone, when he looked at the *bronze serpent*, he lived."

The Imagery of Scripture

The image of the *fiery bronze serpent* is easy to see as an image of the Messiah, for it hung on a *pole* in the same way Jesus would hang upon the cross.

The *serpent* is referred to as "fiery" because it is directly connected to the imagery of the *burning bush*—and how it points to the *burnt offering* that Jesus would provide upon the cross.

In all honesty, the imagery contained in this story is basic; but it is important to let you know that I chose to add it to the book at this point in time for a specific reason. One of the things that I need to do is continually gain your trust that what I am showing you about the Word of God is truth. One step in that equation is using Scripture to support my premise. The book of Acts provides a prime example of this idea. Perhaps the greatest missionary that ever lived, Paul, went to the city of Berea. While he was there, the Bereans did something supreme.

> Acts 17:11 "... they received the word with all readiness, and **searched the Scriptures daily to find out whether these things were so."** (Emphasis mine)

Imagine that. Even Paul had to be accountable to the Word; and if Paul had to do such a thing, so do I.

The imagery of Numbers twenty-one is so relevant because of what we read in the Gospel of John—for Jesus himself pointed to it during his ministry. That revelation in and of itself is staggering, for it gives a clear-cut example of Jesus pointing out the importance of imagery within his holy Word.

This is what he said:

> John 3:14–16 "And as Moses lifted up the *serpent* in the wilderness, even so must the Son of Man be lifted up, that whoever believes in Him should not perish but have eternal life. For God so loved the world that He gave His only begotten Son, that whoever believes in Him should not perish but have everlasting life."

I was stunned when I read that connection for the first time. What may be the best-known verse in the New Testament (John 3:16) is inseparably intertwined with the *bronze serpent* and all the grand imagery of Numbers twenty-one by none other than Jesus himself.

THOSE ANCIENT EYES

Since Jesus himself connected his sacrifice with the *bronze serpent* in John 3:14–16, this imagery has been known for centuries. It therefore should be no surprise that there are noteworthy quotes from the ancient church fathers regarding this imagery.

The first quote, with our imagery inserted, comes from Alcuin of York, who lived from 735–804 AD: "The holy *lamb* . . . Behold, the *bronze serpent* who heals the wounds of the people. Now, you sinner, look with pious thoughts."[1]

Alan of Lille, France, who died in 1203 AD, provides with yet another: "By the *palm tree* we understand the cross of the Lord . . . This is the *tree* on which the *bronze serpent* was suspended."[2]

Before we move on, I think it would be wise to ponder how the details of this story provide a superb summation of the unbelievers in general and their arrogance, stubbornness, and folly. We can almost hear the unbelievers in Numbers twenty-one say to each other, "This is crazy! I don't care what God says, there is no way that looking at and trusting that a *serpent* on a *pole* can save anyone. That's stupid!" Which of course, is exactly what the unbelievers say today, "That's crazy! I don't care what God says, there is no way that looking toward and trusting in Jesus on a cross can save anyone. That's stupid!"

And just like what occurred in Numbers twenty-one, there will be a major consequence for their lack of faith.

But of course, the believers in Numbers twenty-one did not suffer the punishment inflicted upon the unbelievers. God gave them a way out; those who trusted and looked to the image of the *bronze serpent* for their protection would survive. Only the people who "saw" and realized that the *pole* in front of them was actually

---

1. Little and Parker, *The Cloisters Cross*, 172.
2. Little and Parker, *The Cloisters Cross*, 194.

imagery of the *palm tree*, the cross, and the *Tree of Life* all wrapped up into one, would escape God's wrath.

And so it will be for us as well.

Behold, the wonder and awe of how a *serpent* on a *pole* shows anyone and everyone who can see how to be saved.

Before we begin the next section of imagery, we need to peek at two images relevant to that story.

Preface: Bread of Life

> John 6:35, 41 [And Jesus said] "I am the *Bread of Life* . . . I am the *bread* which came down from heaven."

Jesus as the *Bread of Life* is a well-known image. But what some people miss is the imagery connected with the Old Testament blessing of manna. When the children of Israel complained about being hungry in the wilderness after God destroyed the Egyptians, look at their reaction to the special present (the manna as recorded in Exodus 16:12–15) the Lord sent them:

> Numbers 21:5–9 "And the people spoke out against God and against Moses, 'Why have you brought us up out of Egypt to die in the wilderness? For there is no food and no water, and our soul loathes this worthless *bread*.'"

Now let's go back and read Jesus' words as he compares himself with the actual manna given to the children of Israel:

> John 6:58 "This [Jesus himself] is the *bread* which came down from heaven—not as your fathers ate the manna, and are dead. He who eats this *bread* will live forever."

Jesus was making a grand connection: when God fed the children manna (a.k.a. *bread* from heaven) in the desert, he was providing them a prime image of how the real *bread* from heaven (Jesus) would come down to earth and allow all who believe in him to feast upon this *Bread of Life* at Holy Communion.

This imagery is why God had the prophet write:

Isaiah 55:2 "Why do you spend money for what is not *bread*?"

Another obvious reference of *bread* as the Messiah comes from the Master himself:

Matthew 26:26 "And as they were eating, Jesus took *bread*, blessed it and broke it and gave it to the disciples and said, 'Take eat; this is My body.'"

Finally, a passage that gives special symbolism to words we speak on a regular basis—a phrase that from now on should have a special place in our hearts:

Matthew 6:11 "Give us today our daily *bread*."

Daily Jesus! Is there anything greater to ask for in the entire world?

Ponder that imagery for a few moments . . . and then let's move on to—

FISH

Did you ever wonder why you sometimes see a fish symbol on the back of an automobile? I'm sure you have some understanding that the fish is a symbol of Christianity, but do you know why?

The *fish* became a Christian symbol when it was discovered that the Greek word for fish, Ichthys, was an acronym for some of the names and titles of the Messiah. The Greek words, *I*esous *CH*ristos *TH*eou *Y*ios *S*oter, translated into English, mean "Jesus Christ, God's Son, Savior."

And that insight has great implications for our next story.

11

Supreme Food

Free~Broke~Two

I AM CONVINCED THAT PIZZA AND DOUGHNUTS will be considered vegetables in heaven.

It is my favorite meal.

What would you say is yours?

We both might change our minds by the time we are done with this next story.

Let's begin by looking at the selection as it appears in the Bible. We will look at the upcoming miracle as it is recorded in the Gospel of Matthew, but we will use references of the exact same story from the other three Gospels as well.

> Matthew 14:14-20 "And when Jesus went out He saw a great multitude; and He was moved with compassion for them and healed their sick. When it was evening, His disciples came to Him saying . . . 'This is a deserted place, and the hour is already late. Send the multitude away, that they may go into the villages and buy themselves food.' But Jesus said to them, 'They do not need to go away. You give them something to eat.' And they said to Him, 'We have here only five *loaves* and two *fish*.' He said, 'Bring them here to Me.' Then He commanded the multitude to sit down on the grass. And He took the five

loaves and the two *fish*, and looking up to heaven, He blessed and broke and gave the *loaves* to the disciples; and the disciples gave to the multitudes. So they all ate and were filled, and they took up twelve baskets full of the fragments that remained."

Let's break down the pieces and see how they lead to the Messiah:

*Matthew 14:14 "And when Jesus went out He saw a great multitude and He was moved with compassion for them and healed their sick."

We are these sick people that Jesus has compassion on. We seek his healing, and he gladly grants our request because he loves us:

> Mark 2:17 [And Jesus said] "Those who are well have no need of a physician, but those who are sick. I did not come to call the righteous [a.k.a. the arrogant], but sinners to repentance."

*Matthew 14:15 "When it was evening, His disciples came to Him saying . . . 'This is a deserted place, and the hour is already late. Send the multitude away, that they may go into the villages and buy themselves food.'"

Jesus fully understood what was about to happen and knew that the people would not need to go away. Words from the prophet Isaiah were certainly written in connection with this verse from Matthew.

> Isaiah 55:1–2 "Ho! Everyone who thirsts, come to the *waters*. And you who have no money, come and buy and eat. Yes, come, buy *wine* and *milk* without money and without price. Why do you spend money for what is not *bread* and your wages for what does not satisfy? Listen carefully to Me, and eat what is good, and let your soul delight itself in abundance."

The people would not have to go buy food because the *Bread of Life* (and *fish*) would soon be provided for free, just as Isaiah foretold it would; and it would be free because Jesus himself would pay the *price*.

*Matthew 14:16 "But Jesus said to them, 'They do not need to go away. You give them something to eat.'"

No new imagery here, just a foreshadowing of the disciples' future ministry and how they would feed the people with the *Bread of Life* as apostles (and how our pastors do to this very day).

*Matthew 14:19 "Then He commanded the multitude to sit down on the grass. And He took the five *loaves* and the two *fish*, and looking up to heaven, He blessed and broke and gave the *loaves* to the disciples."

To make certain that no one would miss the imagery of this event, Jesus mirrored his actions that would occur on Maundy Thursday:

> Matthew 26:26 "And as they were eating, Jesus took *bread*, blessed it and broke it and gave it to His disciples, and said, 'Take eat, this is My body.'"

The Word cannot make it any clearer: the *loaves* and *fish* that the people would soon receive at the end of Matthew 14:19 were/are an image of Jesus' body presented at the Lord's Supper.

*Matthew 14:20 "So they all ate and were filled."

Being full and the presence of the Savior are inseparably linked:

> Matthew 5:6 [And Jesus said] "Blessed are those who hunger and thirst for righteousness, for they shall be filled."

To be filled with Jesus (and abide in him) is a blessing no words can fully describe.

*Matthew 14:20 "And they took up twelve baskets full of the fragments that remained."

The disciples picked up the leftover pieces because Jesus told them to:

The Imagery of Scripture

> John 6:12 "So when they were filled, He said to His disciples, 'Gather up the fragments that remain, so that nothing is lost.'"

Jesus told his disciples to do this because he wanted all to see and understand that this was incredibly special *food*, not something to be discarded like some common meal. This was a sacred *meal* because it was imagery of abiding with the Savior by eating of his *flesh*.

But alas, the story did not end well; for the people that Jesus fed did not understand his message. Sadly, they did not see things through the eyes of imagery. Instead, they were blind and only saw things through the "eyes" of their stomachs:

> John 6:14–15 "Then those men, when they had seen the sign that Jesus did, said, 'This is truly the Prophet who is come into the world.' Therefore when Jesus perceived that they were about to come and take Him by force to make Him [an earthly] king, He departed . . . "

Jesus so deeply hoped and prayed that these people would heed words he would speak soon after:

> John 6:56 "Whoever eats My *flesh* and drinks My *blood* abides in Me and I in him."

Jesus fed the people an image of his *body* and invited them to abide in and with him. Instead, they closed their eyes and ignored the imagery and the message. May this study help us to avoid making the same mistake.

Something worth noting about the overall focus of this chapter is that some ancient church fathers understood its imagery. Look at what we read in an art book: "Now from the time of the catacombs, the church had always interpreted the miracle of the loaves as a symbol of the Eucharist. This miracle [points to] another miracle: the body of Christ multiplying itself at the same time as the consecrated bread."[1]

---

1. Male, *Religious Art in France: The Twelfth Century*, 424.

Behold, the wonder and awe of five *loaves* and two small *fish*, which brought *life* to the people, but unfortunately was rejected.

Oh hey, I almost forgot—there are three more things. (Okay, I didn't really forget, I just saved them for last.)

First, John 6:3 reveals something else extraordinary about the location of this miracle of supreme *food*. The apostle records that this event took place . . . on a mountain.

And all I can say to that is: could it be any other way?

Second, did you catch how many there were of each item of *food*? There were *five loaves* for the exact same reason that *David* chose *five smooth stones* to slay Goliath—because it pointed to the *five wounds* Christ sustained upon the cross.

That fact alone is enough to leave a person stunned in connection with the overall imagery of this story.

But what about the *fish*?

There were two *fish* because they lead to the Savior as well. (Go figure, right?)

The number two has a variety of images connected with it; but one that is unquestionable is that the number two points to the Messiah's *dual* nature as both true Man and true God. Another reason the church has often connected the number two with Jesus is because he is often referred to as the *Second* Person of the Trinity.

Finally, it's time to see yet another number of imagery within Scripture. Did you notice that the disciples picked up twelve baskets of leftovers? It is a detail that is not to be missed—because in the Bible, twelve is the number of the church. Twelve points to the Old Testament church because of the twelve tribes of Israel, the original family of believers. Twelve also points to the New Testament church because it was organized with Jesus' choosing of the twelve disciples. So, after Jesus fed the people, it makes total sense that this special *food* would be collected into twelve basketfuls—to be redistributed every Sunday across the globe for almost two thousand years and counting.

It is a connection that we cannot and should not miss and one that serves as the perfect way to wrap up this miracle.

12

A Fish & A Coin

Hook~Drachma~Florence

WHAT DO YOU THINK ABOUT TAXES?

Tolerate 'em? Hate 'em?

Jesus had to deal with them, too.

In Matthew 17:24–26, Peter was approached by some men and questioned about why Jesus had not yet paid the yearly tax required of every Jew in order to keep the temple up and running. Before Peter could ask about it, Jesus brought the topic up to him.

In verse twenty-five, Jesus explained to Peter that a royal heir didn't pay taxes to the king since a prince/son was free of such duties. In his words, Jesus was also subtly indicating to Peter how as the Messiah, a "new temple" was now here, and things had changed.

But then something happened.

> Matthew 17:27 [Jesus said to Peter] "Nevertheless, lest we offend them, go to the sea, cast in a hook, and take the *fish* that comes up first. And when you have opened its mouth, you will find *a piece of money*; take that and give it to them for Me and you."

A money-producing fish! How cool is that?

But oh, the imagery behind this event—it's heavenly.

I'm sure you can probably tell where we're headed just by the way the imagery is marked in the preceding verse, but let's break down the details anyway.

The entire theme of these four verses is a *payment price* that needed to be made, and how Jesus told/showed Peter how this *price* would be paid is nothing short of amazing.

The *fish* in this story is an image of Jesus himself. Just as we learned earlier, this *fish* is the Ichthys: Jesus Christ, Son of God, Savior.

Let's look at everything connected with that *fish* and its *payment price*.

*Jesus told Peter to **cast** in a *hook*.

Though it is subtle, Jesus was making a supreme connection when he told Peter to cast something. The Greek word used for Jesus' command is "*ballo*," a common Greek verb, and there is at least one instance where it is inseparably linked with the *payment price* paid by the Messiah.

> Matthew 27:35 "Then they crucified Him, and divided His garments, casting ["*ballo*"] lots, that it might be fulfilled which was spoken by the prophet: 'They divided My garments among them, and for My clothing they cast lots.'"

Subtle, yet supreme.

*Jesus told Peter to cast in a **hook**.

This is another subtle connection, and I think I can present it best to you in the form of a couple of questions:

- What is a *hook* made of?
- How sharp is it at the end?
- What would the *hook* do to the *fish*?

(Why do I think your eyes just lit up a little?)

The answers are that a *hook* is an incredibly sharp thing made from metal that would pierce the *fish*.

The Imagery of Scripture

That should sound familiar.

> John 19:34 "But one of the soldiers pierced His side with a *spear* . . ."

But there's more.

When I looked up the Greek word for *hook* ("*agkistron*") in my Bible Concordance, I found that Matthew 17:27 was the only place in the entire Bible where that Greek word appears. From an imagery point of view, this *hook* was a one-time deal, a one-time event, a one-time *payment price*—exactly like Jesus' atoning sacrifice.

But there's still more.

Take a wild guess how many times the Greek word used in John 19:34 for *spear* ("*logche*") appears in the entire Bible? (Are you smiling?)

Yup—exactly one time—only in John 19:34.

A coincidence? I learned long ago that there is no such thing in God's Word.

Let's head back to Scripture.

*[Jesus said] " . . . take the *fish* that comes up first."

The Greek word Jesus used when he said "take" was "*airo*"—and it is a Greek word that is inseparably linked with the Savior's work of salvation.

Look where else we find that exact same Greek word.

> John 1:29 [And John the Baptizer said] "**Behold**, the *Lamb of God* who takes away ["*airo*"] the sin of the world."

John's words could also be translated as "**Behold**, the *Lamb of God*, who takes up the sins of the world"—a translation that fits perfectly because of how Jesus would take the sins of the world up with him as he climbed into the *palm tree*.

Before we move on, I think this would be the perfect place to state an obvious detail that would be so easy to overlook:

*The *fish* died while yielding up its *payment price*.

A Fish & A Coin

Any fisherman will be able to tell you that when you catch a fish, you can throw it back into the water and it might survive. But that's not always the case; if the *fish* is pierced too severely by the *hook*, it will die no matter what the fisherman does.

And I am convinced, my friends, that that is exactly what happened to the *fish* in our story because the imagery demands that it be so.

I wonder if Peter remembered this event after all was said and done? I can't wait to ask him someday.

*" . . . you will find a *piece of money*."

When Peter opened the mouth of the *fish*, he found a *piece of money*, and while there seems to be a minor disagreement over the actual value of that coin, it is clear that it was a drachma (a Greek coin) that came out of the *fish's* mouth.

And would you care to guess what a drachma was made of in Jesus' day?

The answer is silver. And that leads us here:

> Matthew 26:14–15 "Then one of the twelve, called Judas Iscariot, went to the chief priests and said, 'What are you willing to give me if I deliver Him to you?' And they counted out to him thirty pieces of silver. So from that time he sought opportunity to betray Him."

It could be no other way.

And guess what?

The Greek word for this coin ("*stater*") appears exactly one time in the entire Bible; taking us right back to the idea that the Messiah's atoning sacrifice would be a one-time event.

No more. No less.

So, how is that for a supreme story? A *payment price* paid through a miracle—exactly like the Savior hanging upon a *palm tree* and then rising three days later.

But guess what? (I hope you are smiling!)

The Imagery of Scripture

THE FISHY COIN IN FLORENCE

I'd like you to meet a close friend of mine. He is a man who has improved my vision and who has become inseparably linked with this entire study.

His name is Masaccio. (That's Ma-sach-chee-o)

Even though the story of the fishy coin is not one of the better-known stories in the New Testament, apparently its imagery may have made it appealing to our artist friend.

When Masaccio was hired to paint some of the walls of a chapel located in Florence, Italy, he painted some frescoes (paintings done on wet plaster) that point to a grand connection in regard to our study on the imagery of God's Word.

In the chapel, Masaccio painted an incredible scene: a poignant depiction of Adam and Eve being expelled from the Garden of Eden. In this fresco, Adam covers his face in shame as his wife Eve appears to almost "howl" with sadness and remorse as she hides her nakedness. The emotional depiction of the two characters was something the art world had never seen before and has rarely seen since—even though this scene was painted in the mid to late 1420s AD. It was and is considered by many art critics to be one of the supreme depictions of Paradise lost.

But what many art critics fail to note is that right next to the fresco of Adam and Eve's expulsion is a much larger work depicting the story of "the Fishy Coin."

Masaccio, Brancacci Chapel, 1425–1427, courtesy of Dreamstime.com.

A Fish & A Coin

After everything we just learned in connection with the imagery contained in the story of "the Fishy Coin"—I think it is safe to say that what Masaccio painted was a scene of paradise lost directly next to a scene of imagery that pointed to the *price* it would take to reach paradise regained. (Note: Just in case it matters to you, I should probably let you know that in the long depiction of "the Fishy Coin," Masaccio has painted three separate scenes into one work. In the middle Jesus is shown telling Peter where to find the money. On the left, Peter is at the shore, about to pick up the *fish*. And on the right, Peter is seen giving the money to the tax collector.)

Masaccio.
The Fishy Coin.
Unforgettable!

As we did previously, let's peek at a specific image before we get to the details of the actual story.

Preface: Horn

I mentioned in the story of Cain and *Abel* that firsts can be relevant in Scripture. This is true for the image of a horn in connection with the Savior. The first time the image appears in the Old Testament is in a story we have already looked at.

> Genesis 22:13 "Then Abraham lifted his eyes and looked, and there behind him was a *ram* caught in the thicket by its *horns*."

The first time a horn appears in Scripture, it is directly connected with imagery of the future sacrifice of the Messiah. The first time it appears in the New Testament is in connection with the coming of that *ram*.

> Luke 1:68–69 "Blessed is the Lord God of Israel, for He has visited and redeemed His people, and has raised up a *horn* of salvation for us . . . "

Remember, there is no such thing as a coincidence in God's Word.

Bible scholars have seemingly understood for centuries that a horn is a symbol of power. Now we will see that a *horn* is truly a symbol of that ultimate power. Here are a few other verses from Scripture that use the *horn* as an image of the future Messiah and the power he brings with him.

> II Samuel 22:3 "The God of my strength, in whom I will trust. My shield and the *horn* of my salvation."

> Psalm 148:14 "He has exalted the *horn* of His people."

Armed with that imagery, we are ready for more.

13

Unicorn

Minions~Colors~Reem

Her name is Agnes. No last name. Just Agnes.

When my girls were growing up, we, like many other families, watched quite a few Disney movies. One of our favorites was *Despicable Me*. Years later, we still quote lines from this movie and laugh. In that film, one of the girls in the movie is possibly the cutest character to come from any Disney production—she is the youngest of the three and her name is Agnes. The reason I bring this to your attention is because Agnes carries with her a stuffed toy: a unicorn. And that detail leads us to God's Word. Really.

The journey to write this Bible study began by finding over three hundred images directly connected with the future Messiah. We have seen some of them already: lamb, ram, and fish, to name a few. Of all the specific images of the Messiah I found in Scripture, the *unicorn* was easily one of the biggest surprises. But before we look at where the image is located in the Bible, let's cover a little background on the mysterious creature known as the *unicorn*.

No unicorn has ever been found. It is a mythical beast. Many of the legends that evolved over the centuries revolved around the unicorn as a symbol of the Messiah. For instance:

The Imagery of Scripture

- One legend is that a *unicorn* could only be hunted and killed if the king granted his permission. In that scenario, the king is God the Father, who consented to have his Son, the *unicorn*, hunted and killed. In a unique way, this is a strange summation of a world-famous verse:

  John 3:16 "For God so loved the world . . . "

- Another legend stated that only a virgin was able to subdue a *unicorn* and tame it. The connection with the virgin Mary giving birth to the Son of God in the flesh is apparent.

- Finally, various legends often focused on the physical traits of the *unicorn*: it had a single horn and was considered the most powerful creature on earth. Its horn was often described as being multi-colored: the tip was red (symbolizing blood), the center section was black (representing sin), and the section attached to the head was white (the sin washed away). The body was usually white as well (depicting the sinlessness and purity of the Messiah).

There are other non-Messianic legends connected with the unicorn, but the descriptions we just covered are clearly meant to be seen as an image of the Savior. So, imagine my shock when I found this mythical creature within the Word of God.

But alas, there is a catch, for when I began to dig deeper into this image, I found that all was not as it appeared. The Hebrew word used in the Old Testament is "*reem*," which when translated literally into English means "single horn" or "with but one horn." The translators of the Old King James Version, working in 1611, took things too far and used the word unicorn.

And yet, the imagery fit perfectly. The New King James version translates the Hebrew word as "wild ox," which doesn't seem a perfect fit either because a wild ox would normally have two horns. If the wild ox has one horn, that would be a much better fit. But at least we now understand the Hebrew word used and how it is clearly associated with the Messiah.

Unicorn

Here is where the *"unicorn"* (a.k.a. the one *horn*) appears in the Old Testament according to the 21st Century King James translation.

> Numbers 23:22 "God brings [the children of Israel] out of Egypt. He has strength like a *unicorn*." (Repeated in Numbers 24:8)

> Deuteronomy 33:17 "His Glory is like a firstborn bull and His *horns* like the *horns* of a *unicorn*."

> Job 39:9–10 "Will the *unicorn* be willing to serve you? Will he bed by your manger? Can you bind the *unicorn* in the furrow of your ropes?"

> Psalm 29:6 "He makes them . . . like a young *unicorn*."

> Psalm 92:10 "But my *horn* You have exalted like a *unicorn*."

The Savior of the world as a *unicorn* . . . Completely, utterly amazing!

14

A Wee Little Man
Beethoven~Stature~Jericho

History has provided us with some legendary short people: Napoleon Bonaparte, Charlie Chaplin, Beethoven, and Peter Dinklage... But this biblical wee little man outshines them all.

> Luke 19:1-9 "Then Jesus entered and passed through Jericho. Now **behold**, there was a man named Zacchaeus who was a chief tax collector and he was rich. And he sought to see who Jesus was, but could not because of the crowd, for he was of short stature. So he ran ahead and climbed up into a sycamore *tree* to see Him, for He was going to pass that way. And when Jesus came to the place, He looked up and saw him and said to him, 'Zacchaeus, make haste and come down, for today I must stay at your house.' So he made haste and came down, and received Him joyfully. But when they saw it, they all complained, saying, 'He has gone to be a guest with a man who is a sinner.' Then Zacchaeus stood and said to the Lord, '**Look**, Lord, I give half of my goods to the poor. And if I have taken anything from anyone by false accusation, I restore fourfold.' [And Jesus said to him] 'Today *salvation* has come to this house...'"

A Wee Little Man

In this section of Scripture, Zacchaeus is used as the supreme image of a Messiah follower (a.k.a. a believer). Let's look at the pieces of the puzzle by asking some questions.

1. Where did Zacchaeus go to see Jesus?

    Zacchaeus climbed into a *tree* because that is exactly where Jesus was headed—into a *tree* that was the cross (see Acts 5:30). So, it is quite logical that Zacchaeus, a believer who wanted to see, would head to the exact spot where his Savior had to go: to the *tree*. The end of verse four confirms this idea: "For [Jesus] was going to pass that way."

2. Where did Jesus say he wanted to go?

    Luke 19:5 [And Jesus said] "Zacchaeus . . . come down, for today I must stay at your house."

    Jesus told Zacchaeus to come down from the *tree* because it would only be a temporary stop for the Messiah. Every believer needs to see and understand that the cross (*tree*) was not the final phase of Jesus' visit. He would rise from the dead in an act of triumph, and then He would rule from within his church. The church is where we find the Savior today, which is the reason that Jesus had to go to Zacchaeus's house; for that is exactly where we find our Savior today, in the house of the believer.

3. What was the result of this encounter?

    Read carefully and we quickly realize that the results of this encounter were joy, forgiveness, and salvation—exactly what we should find in the house of God this very day.

4. Why did Zacchaeus have to climb into the *tree* in the first place?

    The 21st Century King James translation tells us that Zacchaeus was "little of stature." I have never thought of this in any other manner than Zacchaeus was short, until I looked at it from a different angle. Zacchaeus did climb the tree in real life because he was short, but the imagery shows

The Imagery of Scripture

us something far more important. The Hebrew equivalent of the Greek word used here for stature is "*qomah.*" In every passage I can locate using this Hebrew word, "high stature" is used as a symbol of arrogance, while "low stature" is used as a symbol of humility. Let's look at two of those passages:

> Isaiah 10:33 "**Behold**, the Lord, the Lord of Hosts will lop off the bough with terror. Those of high stature ["*qomah*"] will be hewn down and the haughty will be humbled."

> Song of Songs 7:7 [And the Messiah said to his bride, the church] "This stature ["*qomah*"] of yours is like a *palm tree.*"

Once again, we return to where this study began. The first passage clearly shows that those of high stature will be cut down to size by the Messiah; and the reference to stature in the Song of Songs shows us that the stature of the church will be like that of the Savior.

This fact is incredibly important to the story of Zacchaeus. Zacchaeus was little of stature for a vital reason, a reason that in and of itself shows the wonder and awe of God's Word: Zacchaeus was little of stature because Jesus had only moments before made a point about the correct attitude of a true believer. Look at what Jesus had said in the previous chapter of the Gospel of Luke.

> Luke 18:13 [And Jesus said in a parable] "And the tax collector, standing afar off, would not so much as raise his eyes to heaven, but beat his breast saying, 'God, be merciful to me a sinner!'"

Take a wild guess what Zacchaeus did for a living: he was a tax collector—and that is why he is said to be little of stature, because he is like us, a repentant sinner. This attitude is confirmed by his act of repentance recorded in verse eight.

To further emphasize the importance of the correct stature, there are two places in the New Testament where a high stature is regarded as a positive thing:

> Luke 2:52 "And Jesus increased in wisdom and stature, and in favor with God and men."
>
> Ephesians 4:13 "Till we all come to the unity of faith and of the knowledge of the Son of God, to a perfect Man, to the measure of the stature of the fullness of Christ."

The message is clear: only Jesus can be of high stature—and this is a stature we will obtain when we meet him in heaven. Why? Because stature is everything in the eyes of God. Stature of purity for his Son, stature of humility (and eventual purity) for his followers.

But there's more.

We need to note where this incredible story took place—in Jericho—and look at what is another name for the city of Jericho:

> II Chronicles 28:15 "So they brought them to their brethren at Jericho, the city of *palm trees*."

Once again, we have come full circle:

> Song of Songs 7:8 [And the Messiah said] "I will go up to the *palm tree*."

(I should probably let you know that right now I am smiling from ear to ear!)

Look at all the things we see: we see the Messiah and a *palm tree*, we see Jesus and a sycamore *tree*, and we see a believer who had the right attitude and was little of stature—as he provided us with an example for the ages. Can we help but stand in awe at the incredible imagery of nine verses from the Gospel of Luke?

15

PERFECT SOUL VISION

Spit~Walking~Fruit

SOMETIMES, THE MOST MEMORABLE STORIES of imagery are the least familiar.

> Mark 8:22-25 "Then [Jesus] came to Bethsaida; and they brought a blind man to Him, and begged Him to touch him. So He took the blind man by the hand and led him out of the town. And when He had spit on his eyes and put His hands on him, He asked him if he saw anything. And he looked up and said, 'I see men like trees, walking.' Then He put His hands on his eyes again and made him look up. And he was restored and saw everyone clearly."

Seeing and understanding God's imagery can increase the wonder and awe of even a miracle, a miracle with intricate details that seem to "scream" imagery. So, the question is: are we listening?

Although at first glance it may seem somewhat basic, much of what Jesus did and said in these verses pointed to the plan of salvation. If there's one thing I have learned throughout this study, it is that nothing in the Bible is there by accident—everything has a purpose. The exact same thing could be said for Jesus' words and actions in the Gospels. So let's look at these verses and "see"—which just happens to be what this story is all about anyway.

Perfect Soul Vision

"So He took the man by the hand and led him out of the town . . . " (Mark 8:23)

Pause and think about this for a second: Jesus could do anything—anywhere, anytime—so why did he take the man outside the town? Why not heal him right there on the spot? What was so important about the location?

Only God knows the answers for sure, but I am convinced that Jesus took the man outside the city because that is how the plan of salvation would be accomplished. How do we know? God tells us so himself.

Hebrews 13:12 tells us that Jesus sanctified the people by suffering outside the gate, which means the exact same thing as being outside the city. That is where all believers need to go to receive their "soul vision"—and that is why I believe Jesus did what he did with the man in Mark 8:23.

Let's break down the remaining details.

"And when He had spit on his eyes . . . " (Mark 8:23)

Yuck, right? Once again, think about this: Jesus is the Son of God, all he had to do was think about healing this man and it would have been done. But he didn't. Instead, he spit and put the spittle on the man's eyes.

But why?

The answer remains the same—because it pointed to the plan of salvation. The Savior would be spit upon and suffer humiliation so that we might be made whole and have our sight restored.

> Matthew 26:65-67 "Then the high priest tore his clothes, saying, 'He has spoken blasphemy! What further need do we have of witnesses? Look, now you have heard His blasphemy! What do you think?' They answered and said, 'He is deserving of death.' Then they spat in His face and beat Him; and others struck Him with the palms of their hands, saying, 'Prophesy to us, Christ! Who is the one who struck You?'"
>
> Matthew 27:29-30 "When they had twisted a crown of thorns, they put it on His head, and a reed in His right

hand. And they bowed the knee before Him and mocked Him, saying, 'Hail, King of the Jews!' Then they spat on Him, and took the reed and struck Him on the head."

Returning to our story, we read:

"And [Jesus] put His hands on him . . . " (Mark 8:23)

This is a no-brainer: the hands that would be pierced upon Calvary are the hands that bring healing and proper vision to each and every believer. So, of course, those same hands were placed upon the man to heal him, for that is how the plan of salvation works.

What happened next is almost beyond words.

After Jesus did the previous three things, he asked the man if he saw anything. The man's reply is nothing short of astounding and is an example of imagery at its grandest.

"I see men like trees, walking." (Mark 8:24)

Before we ponder what the man might have actually seen, let's see why his words are so fitting.

It is intriguing how often in Scripture mankind is referred to as an image of a tree. Here are just a few.

> Isaiah 61:1, 3 [And the Messiah said] "The Spirit of the Lord God is upon Me, because the Lord has anointed Me to preach good tidings to the poor . . . to console them that mourn in Zion, to give them beauty for ashes, the oil of joy for mourning, the garment of praise for the spirit of heaviness; that they may be called trees of righteousness, the planting of the Lord . . . "

> Matthew 7:17–18, 20 [And Jesus said] "Even so, every good tree bears good fruit, but a bad tree bears bad fruit. A good tree doesn't bear bad fruit, nor can a bad tree bear good fruit . . . Therefore by their fruits you will know them."

Good trees (believers) and bad trees (unbelievers) . . . it's as simple as that. So when the man told Jesus that he saw men looking like trees, there can be no doubt whatsoever that Jesus had

Perfect Soul Vision

made the man look through the eyes of imagery. Can you even imagine?

And while God never reveals exactly what the man saw, I'd like us to ponder the possibilities for a minute or two.

As the man looked around, any believer he looked at would have been a good, healthy tree with good fruit upon him or her. This certainly would have included eleven of the disciples. But what did the man see if he looked at Judas Iscariot or any other unbeliever in the crowd (if Jesus allowed them to follow him outside the city)? Surely he would have seen a rotting tree with rotten fruit.

We can almost picture the man crinkling his nose as he turned to look at them.

And that brings us back to the Master. If the man saw people only as trees—

What do you think he saw as he looked at Jesus?

The answer is as easy as any we have given yet in this study: the man would have seen nothing other than the *Tree of Life*! A quote connected with the Cloisters Cross confirms this idea: "The same Lord Jesus, thus becomes for us both Tree and Book of Life..."[1]

I remember when I saw this imagery for the first time at that kitchen table. I stopped and uttered one soft word, "Whoa!" After that, there was much silence in an attempt to comprehend what that man actually saw.

Before the man could say anything more, Jesus finished the job. But as he placed his hands once again on the man's eyes, he did something else that was incredibly important—he had the man look up.

This direction was already implied in verse twenty-four, when the man looked up and saw the trees, but what does the direction mean?

There is a section of the Old Testament that gives us a clue.

> Psalm 40:11–12 "Do not withhold Your tender mercies from me, O Lord; let Your lovingkindness and Your

---

1. Little and Parker, *The Cloisters Cross*, 190.

truth continually preserve me. For innumerable evils have surrounded me, my iniquities have overtaken me, so that I am not able to look up . . . "

Sin keeps a person from looking up toward God and his heavenly kingdom, but that all changed with the coming of the Savior, for with his coming (and eventual sacrifice) all believers can now look up as the forgiven children they (and we) truly are. They are restored (see Mark 8:25) in the eyes of the Father.

Jesus' atoning sacrifice brings with it perfect soul vision to all those who look through the eyes of faith, which is exactly why the last thing God tells us regarding the miracle in Mark eight is this:

"And [the man] saw everyone clearly." (Mark 8:25)

This certainly means more than just 20/20 vision; this means the man not only saw the men around him as good trees or bad trees, he saw Jesus for who he truly was—the *Son of God* and the *fruit* from the *Tree of Life*. And that, my friends, is the very definition of perfect "soul vision."

May we continue to desire to learn to see as this man was blessed to see.

Men like trees . . . Can you even imagine?

Before we leave this grand story and its equally impressive imagery, there is one more verse from Scripture that we need to consider—and I have been saving it for this very moment.

> Jeremiah 11:19 "But I was like a docile *lamb* brought to the *slaughter*, and I did not know that they had devised schemes against Me, saying, 'Let us destroy the *Tree* [of *Life*] with its *fruit*, and let us cut Him off from the land of the living, that His name may be remembered no more.'"

Besides being able to connect this single verse from the prophet Jeremiah with a multitude of stories that we have covered previously (see Numbers 13:27 as one example), what we need to see here is that the Hebrew word used in Jeremiah 11:19 for the *fruit* of the Savior is *"lechem."* It is a Hebrew word that is normally translated as *bread*—and that means that the *fruit* of this verse is the exact same as the *Bread of Life*.

So, what did the blind man see when he looked at Jesus: *fruit* or *bread* . . . or *both*? All I know for sure is that I plan on talking to him as soon as I enter heaven myself—because I cannot wait to hear what he has to tell me.

Men like trees . . .

Paul Cezanne, ***Large Pine and Red Earth*****, 1895–97, Hermitage, courtesy of Dreamstime.com.**

. . . Can you even imagine?

16

Water & Wine

Friends~One Source~Spear

Favorites remain and persist in the mind.

After thousands upon thousands of hours spent working on this Bible study, I found that I kept returning to two specific sections of Scripture. As time passed, I came to look at those two sections as close friends. The first verse was obvious, for it was where this journey began in the first place.

> Song of Songs 7:8 "I will go up to the *palm tree*, I will take hold of its *branches*."

We will get to the other verse soon. I promise.

> John 2:1-11 "On the third day there was a wedding in Cana of Galilee, and the mother of Jesus was there. Now both Jesus and His disciples were invited to the wedding. And when they ran out of wine, the mother of Jesus said to Him, 'They have no wine.' Jesus said to her, 'Woman, what does your concern have to do with Me? My hour has not yet come.' His mother said to the servants, 'Whatever He says to you, do it.' Now there were set there six waterpots of stone, according to the manner of purification of the Jews, containing twenty or thirty gallons apiece. Jesus said to them, 'Fill the waterpots

with water.' And they filled them up to the brim. And He said to them, 'Draw some out now, and take it to the master of the feast.' And they took it. When the master of the feast had tasted the water that was made wine, and did not know where it came from (but the servants who had drawn the water knew), the master of the feast called the bridegroom. And he said to him, 'Every man at the beginning sets out the good wine, and when the guests have well drunk, then the inferior. You have kept the good wine until now!' This beginning of signs Jesus did in Cana of Galilee, and manifested His glory; and His disciples believed in Him."

The first thing we need to note comes from the sixth verse.

> John 2:6 "Now there were set there six waterpots of *stone*, according to the manner of purification of the Jews . . . "

Think about the implications of that verse for a moment.

- The *water* Jesus used in this miracle was there for purifying and making someone clean—or, from an imagery point of view, the washing away of sin.
- That *water* would be forever inseparably linked with *wine*.
- The *water* and *wine* both came from one source.

When Jesus turned *water* into *wine*, he was showing the world how those liquids would become inseparably linked with the plan of salvation and the purification of each and every believer. And once we realize that for almost two thousand years the Christian church has taught that *wine* is directly connected to the blood of Jesus (at Holy Communion), where we are headed next should be no surprise whatsoever.

> John 19:34 "But one of the soldiers pierced His side with a *spear* and immediately *blood* and *water* came out."

The medical field can explain to us why *blood* and *water* came out of Jesus when his side was pierced, but now we understand from an imagery point of view why that was as well: because it pointed to nowhere else but the sacraments of Baptism (the *water*)

The Imagery of Scripture

and the Lord's Supper (the *wine*). And just in case you are wondering where the *bread* of Communion was in that scenario—it was hanging on the cross!

And that imagery is why John 19:34 has become a friend that will never leave me. Ever.

17

The Twenty-third Psalm
Grass~Fatten~Two

It's time for a confession: I looked forward to writing this chapter for a long, long time.

The best place to start is with the words themselves. Read the poetry of Psalm twenty-three like you are reading it for the first time.

> "The Lord is my Shepherd; I shall not want.
> He makes me to lie down in green pastures;
> He leads me beside the still waters.
> He restores my soul;
> He leads me in the paths of righteousness for His Name's sake.
> Yea, though I walk through the valley of the shadow of death, I will fear no evil;
> For You are with me;
> Your rod and Your staff they comfort me.
> You prepare a table before me in the presence of my enemies;
> You anoint my head with oil;
> My cup runs over.
> Surely goodness and mercy shall follow me all the days of my life;
> And I will dwell in the house of the Lord forever."

Now let's look at the psalm through the eyes of imagery.

The Imagery of Scripture

*"The Lord is my *shepherd*." (Psalm 23:1)

This phrase rolls off our tongues so easily that at times we probably don't fully comprehend the imagery surrounding it. Sheep are some of the dumbest animals on the face of the earth. If the lead sheep walks off a cliff and falls to its death, the other sheep will follow. A sheep that wanders off from the herd has about zero chance of ever reaching home.

In short, a sheep is doomed without its *shepherd*, and that is why we read in the New Testament:

> John 10:10-11, 14-16 [And Jesus said] "The thief does not come except to steal, and to kill, and to destroy. I have come that [the sheep] may have life, and that they may have it more abundantly. I am the *good shepherd*. The *good shepherd* gives His life for the sheep . . . I am the *good shepherd*; and I know My sheep, and am known by My own. As the Father knows Me, even so I know the Father; and I lay down My life for the sheep. And other sheep I have which are not of this fold [that's Gentiles like us!]; them also I must bring, and they will hear My voice; and there will be one flock and one *shepherd*!"

Jesus is our *shepherd* . . . and may we never forget it.

With that introduction completed, I think it would be wise for us to establish the crux of the rest of this chapter before we go any further. Understanding that focal point will allow us to better see the imagery that follows. Here it is in a nutshell:

> The entire focus of Psalm twenty-three is on how Jesus will lead his flock back to paradise. Adam and Eve were driven from Eden for their rebellion (see Genesis 3:24), but the *good shepherd* wants more than anything to bring us back home.

Let's see if I can show you why this is so.

*"He makes me lie down in green pastures." (Psalm 23:2)

For an insight regarding the pasture, we need to return to the New Testament.

The Twenty-third Psalm

> John 10:7, 9 [Then Jesus said] "**Most assuredly,** I say to you, I am the *door* of the sheep . . . I am the *door*. If anyone enters by Me, he will be saved, and will go in and out and find pasture."

Adam and Eve were barred from reentering the door into Eden after the fall—now Jesus wants to rectify that scenario. The pasture is in paradise—and Jesus is the *door* we must pass through to enter that lush land.

There is another section of Scripture that we have already covered that connects directly with this imagery.

> Matthew 14:19 "Then He commanded the multitude to sit down on the grass. And He took the five *loaves* and the two *fish*, and looking up to heaven, He blessed and broke and gave the *loaves* to the disciples."

In the feeding of the five thousand, Jesus, the *good shepherd*, had the people sit down on the grass because it provided imagery of how they were the flock and he was their true *shepherd* who will lead them to green pastures. And what followed? A *meal* that will continue to be eaten in paradise for all eternity.

*"He leads me beside the still *waters*." (Psalm 23:2)

The still *waters* lead to paradise because these are the *waters of life* that only Jesus can provide (see John 4:5–15). These *waters* are "still" because they are not turbulent or dangerous. They are refreshing and life-giving. And where will we find *waters* like that for all eternity?

> Revelation 22:1–2 "And he showed me a pure river of *water of life*, clear as crystal, proceeding from the throne of God and of the *lamb*. In the middle of its street, and on either side of the river, was the *Tree of Life* . . . "

What was John looking at in this final vision of Scripture? Paradise, of course.

*"He restores my soul." (Psalm 23:3)

Once again, I think we are at one of those phrases that so many people say without truly contemplating what it means. What does it mean to restore a soul? For the best explanation, look where else God uses the exact same Hebrew word.

> Exodus 4:6–7 [And the Son said to Moses at the *burning bush*] "'Now put your hand in your bosom.' And he put his hand in his bosom, and when he took it out, **behold**, his hand was leprous, like snow. And He said, 'Put your hand in your bosom again.' So he put his hand in his bosom again, and drew it out of his bosom, and **behold**, it was restored like his other flesh."

These two verses from the fourth chapter of Exodus point to how the *burning bush*, which is an image of the cross, would be responsible for taking away the leprosy/sin that infects each and every believer and how that act would one day restore the believer to how things were in Eden before the fall.

*"He leads me in the paths of *righteousness*." (Psalm 23:3)

Prior to this study, I would instantly have thought of paths of righteousness as a general phrase instead of an image of the Savior. But once I learned to look through the eyes of imagery, that changed. The path or way to heaven (a.k.a. paradise) has to contain *righteousness*—for that is the only way back to God. But look at how those things suddenly become him.

> John 14:6 [And Jesus said] "I am the *way* [a.k.a. the path], the truth, and the life. No one comes to the Father except through Me."

> Malachi 4:1–2 "For **behold**, the day is coming, burning like an oven, and all the proud, yes, all who do wickedly will be stubble. And the day which is coming will burn them up . . . But to you who fear My name, The *Sun of Righteousness* shall arise with healing in His *wings* . . ."

The Twenty-third Psalm

Another Old Testament passage subtly connects the idea of the Savior as *righteousness* with paradise/Eden—a place known for its trees.

> Isaiah 61:1, 3 [And the Messiah said] "The Spirit of the Lord God is upon Me, because the Lord has anointed Me to preach good tidings to the poor; He has sent Me to heal the brokenhearted to proclaim liberty to the captives, and the opening of the prison to those who are bound . . . that they may be called trees of *righteousness*, the planting of the Lord, that He may be glorified."

Trees of *righteousness*? I don't know about you, but I'm thinking of a certain blind man with 20/20 soul vision. (And yes, I have an enormous grin on my face.)

Before we move on, let's peek at one more Bible verse that puts a new spin on Jesus as *righteousness*.

> Matthew 5:6 [And Jesus said] "Blessed are those who hunger and thirst for *righteousness*, for they shall be filled."

Where do we get in line for that happy meal?

*"Yea, though I walk through
the valley of the shadow of death,
I will fear no evil." (Psalm 23:4)

Because of everything Jesus did for us, we can enter the valley of death without fear or dread. God's judgment of wrath and calamity awaits only those who have rejected him; but that's not us—which is why we can walk through that valley with all boldness and confidence. The Hebrew word used here for evil ("*ra*") can also be translated as calamity or harm, a translation that fits perfectly with the overall imagery.

*"For You are with me,
Your *rod* and Your *staff*
they comfort me." (Psalm 23:4)

The Imagery of Scripture

God makes it clear—we need not fear death because of the Savior's *rod* and *staff*. To get the full impact of their imagery I think it would be best if we asked a basic question:

What are a *rod* and a *staff*?

A *staff* was a longer piece of wood, sometimes with a slight hook at the end used to retrieve sheep who found themselves in difficult positions (like falling into a ditch or rock crevice). A *rod* was a shorter piece, often used as a club or weapon. From an imagery point of view, the answer is that a *rod* and a *staff* are two pieces of *wood*, with one being longer (the *staff*) than the other (the *rod*). So, if we merged the *rod* and *staff* of the Savior, we could get an object that looks something like this:

Now do you see why we need not fear the valley of death because of the Savior's *rod* & *staff*? (I'm wondering if your mouth is hanging open like mine did the first time I saw that imagery.)

The fact that these two *sticks* of the Messiah comfort all believers is equally important. Look where else we find the exact same Hebrew word used for "comfort" in Psalm 23:4.

The Twenty-third Psalm

Isaiah 51:3 "For the Lord will comfort Zion, He will comfort all her waste places; He will make her wilderness **like Eden**, and her desert **like the garden of the Lord**..." (Emphasis mine)

Are you kidding me?
Any questions?
And look at what follows that supreme imagery of the cross and the Messiah's sacrifice.

*"You prepare a table before me
in the presence of my enemies." (Psalm 23:5)

A table? How much do you want to bet that there's some tasty *bread* on it?

*"You anoint my head with *oil*." (Psalm 23:5)

Try not to laugh, but the Hebrew word used for "anoint" in this verse is "*dashen*," a Hebrew word that usually means "to fatten." So, the verse could read:

"You fatten my head with *oil*."

The oil that God fattens our heads with is none other than the *oil* of the Messiah. We learn such a detail from a section of Scripture we have already encountered.

Isaiah 61:1, 3 [And the Messiah said] "The Spirit of the Lord God is upon Me, because the Lord has anointed Me to preach good tidings to the poor; He has sent Me to heal the brokenhearted to proclaim liberty to the captives, and the opening of the prison to those who are bound... to console those who mourn in Zion, to give them beauty for ashes, the *oil* of joy for mourning, the garment of praise for the spirit of heaviness; that they may be called trees of *righteousness*, the planting of the Lord, that He may be glorified."

The Imagery of Scripture

*"My cup runs over." (Psalm 23:5)

Since our table will have never-ending *bread* on it, how much do you want to bet that our cup will overflow with some world-class *wine*? (Would you like a red from Bordeaux or perhaps Napa, or would you prefer a white from the Mosel or maybe Alsace?)

*"Surely *goodness* and *mercy* shall follow me all the days of my life." (Psalm 23:6)

In this brief phrase, we witness a miracle of God: the Messiah leads and he follows all at the same time. He leads us into the Promised Land that is paradise, and he follows us to make sure we are safe. You might say he has both ends covered.

But there's one more thing we need to note regarding this section from Psalm twenty-three. Do you remember what we learned in an earlier chapter was the number of the Messiah? The answer is two, mainly because Jesus was both 1.) true man and 2.) true God (in addition to being the Second Person of the Trinity). Well, look once again at how many things follow us all the days of our life: two!

Goodness and *mercy*!

A grand insight that would be so easy to miss.

*"And I will dwell in the house of the Lord forever." (Psalm 23:6)

After Judgment Day—after all is said and done—where will God's house be found? The answer is a place called paradise; and our *good shepherd* will welcome us with a smile for the ages, and we, the sheep, will run to him like we have never run before.

Behold, the wonder and awe of Psalm twenty-three, one of the best-known sections in all of Scripture, and one that I can only hope and pray was/is as amazing for you as it was/is for me now that I see and understand its imagery.

Preface: The Fifth Gospel

Some of the ancient church fathers were so enthralled with the prophet Isaiah that they sometimes referred to his book as the "fifth Gospel." St. Jerome (347–420 AD) thought that it looked more like Isaiah was telling the story of the past rather than the future.

Equipped with that insight, let's peek at details that come from the beginning of Isaiah's book.

18

The Ox & The Donkey
King~Trough~Cave

> Isaiah 1:3 "The ox knows its *owner* and the donkey its *master's crib*."

THESE ELEVEN WORDS FROM THE THIRD VERSE of Isaiah's book had a special meaning to more than a few of the ancient church fathers. They believed that the two humble creatures mentioned in this verse pointed to you and me as the family of all believers. Since only the humble have faith, what two animals of imagery would be better to use than the humble ox and donkey?

The ancient church fathers couldn't decide which animal represented the Old Testament Jewish believers and which represented the New Testament Gentile believers (I had a student who said he sure hoped we were the ox!), but they saw the two divisions of God's family, nonetheless.

Francis of Assisi (who lived in Italy from 1181–1226 AD) is generally credited with creating the first manger scene. If we read the Gospels of Matthew and Luke carefully, we see that the animals we find in every manger scene today are never mentioned. But St. Francis apparently inserted the ox and donkey mainly because of what we read in Isaiah 1:3, because it tells us that these two animals are connected with their *master's crib*.

Here is an example from the art world.

Gerard David, *The Nativity with Donors and Sanits Jerome and Leonard*, 1510–15, courtesy of the Metropolitan Museum of Art, New York City

But that is just the beginning.

THE MANGER

There is something else we need to see in connection with Isaiah 1:3. Over the years I have heard various pastors mention some of what will follow; but when I saw this imagery for the first time, it was all new to me. To fully understand the imagery connected with Isaiah 1:3, we need to open our Bibles to the New Testament Gospels.

> Luke 2:7 "And she brought forth her firstborn Son and wrapped Him in swaddling cloths and laid Him in a *manger*, because there was no room for them in the inn."

Is there a Christian who doesn't know this verse? It is read by pastors every December and spoken by countless numbers of

The Imagery of Scripture

children at Christmas programs. But how many Christians see and understand the imagery connected with these words?

Amazingly (and I do not use that word lightly), the birth of Jesus revealed the entire plan of salvation and how it would be accomplished.

Let me explain by asking two questions:

- What does it mean that Jesus was laid in a *manger*?
- What exactly is a *manger*?

A *manger* is a feeding trough for animals. When the Savior of the world was laid in a *manger*, God was showing the entire world that the humble of faith (a.k.a. the ox and the donkey of Isaiah 1:3) would eat and feast upon that very Savior.

This entire idea is reinforced when we look back at the first chapter of Isaiah.

> Isaiah 1:2–3 "Hear, O heavens, and give ear, O earth! For the Lord has spoken: 'I have nourished [a.k.a. fed] and brought up children, and they have rebelled against Me; the ox knows its *owner* and the donkey its *master's crib* . . .'"

But there is another connection to be made regarding this feasting that is enough to make a person shake his/her head in wonder.

Did you ever consider why God decided in his infinite wisdom that his Son had to be born in Bethlehem? Besides the fact that the prophet Micah wrote through inspiration that it would be so (in Micah 5:2), the incredible thing to note is that the name Bethlehem means "the house or place of *bread!*"

Imagine that—*living bread* that came down from heaven, laid in a *manger* so that the oxen and donkeys (that's us) could feast upon him for all eternity.

Exactly how cool is that?

ALTAR

The art world and ancient church fathers clearly understood this imagery. Look at what we read in an art book on the grand cathedral in Chartres, France (with our imagery inserted): "At birth, the Christ Child is placed not in a homely *manger* but... sacramentally upon an altar . . . [an altar] supported by two sculpted columns to symbolize that His *blood* and *flesh* are present in the eucharist."[1]

While the stained-glass window at Chartres places Jesus in an actual *manger*, the Klosterneuburg ambo gets to the very heart of the imagery.

Nicholas of Verdun, *The Klosterneuburg ambo*, 1171–81, courtesy of Klosterneuburg abbey.

Look closely and notice that Nicholas of Verdun has depicted the Christ Child as if he were placed on that biblical-like, sacrificial altar with legs instead of the normal *manger*.

Pssst . . . Did you notice the ox and the donkey located right above the *manger*?

1. Miller, *Chartres Cathedral*, 32.

The Imagery of Scripture

And here's something else we need to think about:

What was a *manger* made of two thousand years ago?

It seems there are two distinct possible answers. The first is that the *manger* would have been made of wood, and I assume that imagery requires no explanation whatsoever. But *mangers* of that time period were often merely a trough carved or chiseled out of large stone or rock; and that imagery leads us to a new and grand potential insight. I learned long ago that not only is the birth of Jesus inseparably linked with the cross, so is the tomb. That may sound far too obvious, but it is a vital piece of information because it still leads us back to that *palm tree*.

If baby Jesus was laid upon stone instead of wood, then what we suddenly have is an image of how he would lay in the tomb after the crucifixion. Stone? Wood? Either way, we return to the cross and its aftermath.

While we're on the general topic, we should also note something else about the stable Jesus was born in. The Bible never specifically uses the word stable, but we are probably right in assuming it was a stable based on the facts: 1.) that is where you would find a *manger* and 2.) there was no room in the inn.

But what we need to do is clarify the word stable. If I understand things correctly, a stable in the Middle East isn't like a stable in America. Wood was seemingly way too precious a commodity in the Middle East to be used on an animal shed, so instead, most people kept their animals under rocky overhangs or in . . . are you ready for this? . . . or in a cave!

If . . . and I repeat if, Jesus was born in a cave, there can be no doubt that God provided a superb image of how his Son would one day rest in a tomb "carved out of the rock"—something that Scripture tells us indeed occurred.

> Matthew 27:59-60 "When Joseph had taken the body, he wrapped it in a clean linen cloth, and laid it in his new tomb which he had hewn out of the rock; and he rolled a large stone against the door of the tomb, and departed."

The art world understood this insight. Look at the following masterpiece by an Italian artist known as Giorgione (George-gee-oh-nee)—and look where he depicts the nativity of Jesus and the adoration of the shepherds:

Giorgione, *The Adoration of the Shepherds*, 1505–10, courtesy National Gallery of Art, Washingon.

... at a *cave*!

Makes a person wonder.

Oh, and did you notice the ox and the donkey inside the cave to the right of Mary and Joseph?

This idea is further enhanced by what else we read regarding the birth of Jesus.

> Luke 2:7 "And she brought forth her firstborn Son and wrapped Him in *swaddling cloths* and laid Him in a *manger*, because there was no room for them in the inn."

Once again, we need to ask ourselves a question:

What are *swaddling cloths*?

The Imagery of Scripture

Swaddling cloths are narrow strips of cloth bound and wrapped tightly around the body. Sound vaguely familiar? Look at what we read in the Gospels.

> John 19:40 "Then [Joseph of Arimathea and Nicodemus] took the body of Jesus, and bound it in *strips of linen* . . . "

Imagine that—Jesus' *swaddling cloths* used at his birth pointed to the *strips of linen* used at his burial.

Before we wrap up this chapter, let's take one last look at the nativity scene painted by Gerard David more than five hundred years ago.

When we peek back at the painting, we see that in the lower right corner of the central panel is a sheaf or stalk of wheat. And what can wheat be turned into? Edible *bread*! Note how the placement of this "future *bread*" echoes almost perfectly the body position of the Christ Child in the *manger*.

And what rests across this food-to-be? A *staff*.

To the immediate left of this wheat and wood is a beautifully depicted wicker basket that contains the *swaddling cloths*, which point to the burial shroud to come. Birth and death. Inseparable.

A masterpiece of imagery in every way.

It was all but impossible not to smile, when, after I penned the above words, I read the following in an art book that contains a picture of David's painting:

> "Despite the joyful moment depicted, the expressions and gestures of the figures strike a somber tone, in recognition of the fact that his birth will culminate in Christ's sacrifice for the redemption of mankind. This meaning is reinforced by . . . the eucharistic symbolism of the *sheaf of wheat* ("I am *the bread of life*"), and the basket with the *swaddling cloth*, which suggests the winding cloth used to prepare the dead Christ for burial."[2]

You know what? I have never been able to look at a *manger* scene again without thinking about the details recorded in this chapter . . . And it makes me smile every time.

---

2. Ainsworth and Christiansen, *From Van Eyck to Brueghel*, 302–04.

Epilogue

We will pause there. There is more. Much more. But, God willing, that will be for another day. My goal in writing this first book was simple: to provide you with a small taste of this thing called imagery and show you a glimpse of how wondrous it is within the Word.

It is undeniable that imagery is a viable way of studying the Scriptures. Jesus' words in John 3:14–15 deliver the proof. But one must be careful not to let the imagination run wild. True imagery points us to Jesus and his atoning sacrifice. Imagery that takes the focus away from Calvary is not true imagery.

This book of highlights was meant to whet your appetite. There is so much more to see and digest. There is so much that I would love the opportunity to share with you.

I can only hope and pray that you are intrigued enough to give me the chance.

> "Oh, taste and see that the Lord is good . . . "
> Psalm 34:8

Bibliography

Ainsworth, Margaret W., and Keith Christiansen. *From Van Eyck to Brueghel: Early Netherlandish Paintings in the Metropolitan Museum of Art.* New York: Metropolitan Museum Art, 1998.

Finaldi, Gabriele. *The Image of Christ.* London: National Gallery, 2000.

Hoving, Thomas. *King of the Confessors.* New York: Simon and Schuster, 1981.

Little, Charles T., and Elizabeth Parker. *The Cloisters Cross: Its Art and Meaning.* New York: Metropolitan Museum Art, 1994.

Male, Emile. *Religious Art in France: The Twelfth Century.* New Jersey: Princeton University Press, 1978.

Miller, Malcolm. *Chartres Cathedral.* New York: Riverside, 1996.

Minne-Seve, Viviane, and Herve Kergall. *Romanesque and Gothic France: Art and Architecture.* New York: Harry N. Abrams, 2000.

Peterson, Manning. "What Was the Biblia Pauperum?" *The Internet Biblia Pauperum*, August 8, 2001. http://amasis.com/biblia/what.html.

Saint Augustine. *The City of God.* Translated by Marcus Dods. New York: Random House, 1993.

www.ingramcontent.com/pod-product-compliance
Lightning Source LLC
Chambersburg PA
CBHW071625170426
43195CB00038B/2122